EVERYDAY
WISDOM

1,001 Expert Tips for Hikers

EVERYDAY WISDOM

1,001 Expert Tips for Hikers

by Karen Berger

BACKPACKER
THE MAGAZINE OF WILDERNESS TRAVEL

Published by
The Mountaineers
1001 SW Klickitat Way, Suite 201
Seattle, WA 98134

© 1997 by *BACKPACKER* magazine
33 East Minor Street
Emmaus, PA 18098

First printing 1997, second printing 1997, third printing 1998

Published simultaneously in Great Britain by Cordee, 3a DeMontfort Street, Leicester, England, LE1 7HD

Manufactured in the United States of America

Edited by Kris Fulsaas
Cover design by Helen Cherullo
Book design by Alice Merrill
Book layout by Ani Rucki
Typography by Jennifer Shontz
Illustrations by Dawn Peterson

Cover photograph: © John Page, Alaska Stock
Frontispiece: © Karen Berger/Daniel R. Smith

Library of Congress Cataloging-in-Publication Data
Berger, Karen, 1959–
    Backpacker's everyday wisdom : 1001 expert tips for hikers / by Karen
Berger.
        p.   cm.
    ISBN 0-89886-523-9
    1. Hiking. 2. Backpacking. I Backpacker. II. Title. III. Title: Everyday
wisdom.
GV 199.5.B466   1997
796.51—DC21   97-25591
                                                                CIP

Contents

"I remembered a Swahili sailor..." / 7

CHAPTER 1
BACKPACKING BASICS / 11
   What You Need to Know Before You Go

CHAPTER 2
FOOD AS FUEL / 34
   Planning Menus to Stoke Your Stomach

CHAPTER 3
ON THE TRAIL / 57
   Prepped for Adventure

CHAPTER 4
THE COMFORT ZONE / 74
   Making Your Home in the Woods

CHAPTER 5
AT THE CHUCKWAGON / 99
   Backcountry Cookcraft

CHAPTER 6
WEATHER / 109
   How to Laugh at Stormy Skies

CHAPTER 7
HEALTHY HIKER / 127
   Dealing with Bumps, Bites, and Blisters

CHAPTER 8

WATER / 161

　Finding It, Treating It, and Avoiding Parasitic Distress

CHAPTER 9

FIELD REPAIRS / 175

　Beyond Saftey Pins and Duct Tape

CHAPTER 10

BETWEEN TRIPS / 186

　A Little Maintenance Prevents a Lot of Mildew

Index / 201

"I remembered a Swahili sailor . . ."

THE ONLY WARNING was a sort of lift in the air pressure, like the breath a sprinter takes before the gun goes off. Then the raindrops started, the big splatting kind that explode against the ground like water balloons on a hot summer day.

At exactly that minute, the stove sputtered once, then stopped. The rain made a metallic splash on the cookpot lid. I removed it and put my finger in the water, which was sort of hot. Well, lukewarm.

We had hoped the white gas would last until the next big town. It hadn't. All we had was a plastic bottle of something called *alcool à brûler*, the only fuel available in the tiny French town in this remote part of the Pyrenees. The container it came in had a picture of a stove on it. The text of the bottle contained a couple of optimistic cognates: *combustible*, *inflammable*, and *dangereux*. We had been calling it "the bomb." We had been hoping it would work.

It didn't.

Ever notice how your stove never conks out on a sunny day when you're camped near a fire ring with a leftover supply of dry wood?

It rained harder. And forget about dry wood—or any kind of wood. This far above tree line, the only wood in the vicinity was the spent matchsticks from trying to light the stove.

I was hungry. My hiking partners were hungry. Hardly life-threatening, but distinctly unpleasant.

And then I remembered a Swahili sailor who had shown me how to make an efficient little fire on an African beach. I remembered that when I hiked the Continental Divide, I had read about the settlers of the Oregon Trail, who used buffalo dung to cook on. I also knew that we had at least one quick-cooking no-fuss meal in our food bags, and

▲   7   ▲

plenty more matches in a waterproof container. And there were cow pies in the area.

I made a three-stone perch for my pot, poured the *alcool à brûler* on a few broken-up dried cowpats, lit a match, and 15 minutes later, I got a hero's welcome when I presented my hiking partners with a completely hot, completely cooked dinner.

Experience in the woods teaches that little things count. My cow-pie triumph was the result of learning from others (the African sailor and the American pioneers) and adapting their tricks to my predicament. It also demonstrated the value of good preparation (we had the quick-cooking meal available for just such an emergency) and the consequences of bad preparation (we should have taken the trouble to test the new fuel before we got out in the field).

Experienced hikers know that their most important piece of gear isn't some nifty doodad—it's the gray matter they carry in their heads. Whether it's a dung fire, fixing a broken tent pole, finding a more comfortable way to get yourself down a scree slope, or the simple pleasure of having just exactly what you need in your pack and nothing more, there are a thousand secrets, surprises, tips, and techniques that can make your backcountry experience more enjoyable. In order to make 40 pounds of gear meet all your needs, you've got to choose your gear well and know how to make the best of it. Creativity and improvisation will carry you a long way when you've got a stove that won't light, a water filter that won't pump, and a hiking partner who won't quit complaining. But a little know-how and some basic preparation can make a whole lot of backcountry problems just disappear.

Sometimes it seems that the outdoor industry thinks that the way to make yourself comfortable in the backcountry is to spend money on and carry the weight of a lot of high-tech gizmos. But after more than 10,000 miles of backpacking, I've come to a few simpler, less expensive, and lighter-weight conclusions: The secret of comfortable outdoor life is preparing for the predictable, and solving problems by avoiding them. A light pack means comfort on the trail. Having exactly what you need means comfort in camp. And a few tried and true tricks up your sleeve can make all the difference when things don't go exactly as planned.

To write this book, I've relied on my own 10,000 or so miles of backpacking experience, as well as the experience of Dan Smith, my husband and hiking partner, who has tromped with me all over the world. I've also learned from my many other hiking partners, as well as from casual encounters with other backpackers. And I continue to learn.

One of the most important lessons: There are as many techniques as hikers. Over the years, *BACKPACKER* magazine readers have written in with advice on hundreds of ways to do things, and I could probably fill another book with all the advice I left out of this one. I tried to choose tips that would be useful for most people in most circumstances, and to share ideas that would make a marked difference in backcountry comfort and safety. I also leaned heavily toward practical ideas that experienced backpackers routinely put into practice.

But this isn't a book to memorize and quote from; it's a book to share ideas and get you thinking about what will work for you. Look at it as a menu, a smorgasbord of techniques to ease the way and maybe help you out in a pinch. Some of the ideas may seem superfluous or unnecessary to you. Some of them require extra gear—only a little bit, and always lightweight, but with 1,001 tips, the pounds add up. Some of them won't fit your hiking style. Some are so obvious, you might find yourself wondering—as I often have—"Why didn't I think of that years ago?" And if one of these days I meet you on the trail and you tell me that something you read in this book helped you fix the stove, pitch the tent, find your way, or simply luxuriate that little bit more, it will have done its job.

How much can you carry? Aim for no more than one-fourth of your body weight—less if you haven't worked out for a while.
(Photo: Jeff Scher ©ERG)

CHAPTER I

BACKPACKING BASICS

What You Need to Know Before You Go

BACKPACKERS WILL TELL you a thousand reasons they take to the woods. Your reasons for heading out can range from aesthetics to exercise, from private time to family time, from stargazing to view-chasing, but whatever they are, you'll judge the success of your trip the same way when you get back. If everyone comes out safe and smiling and eager to do it again, it's been a success.

Simple, isn't it? Well, maybe not that simple. Because, as any experienced hiker can tell you, the secret to a happy hike lies, at least in part, in your preparation. It lies in deciding what kind of trip you want and planning for it. It means having the right gear so that you're comfortable in camp—and not too much of it, so you're comfortable carrying it on the trail. It means dealing with the unexpected, watching glorious sunsets, diving into the perfect swimming hole, and having just the right item in your repair kit to repair that blown-out tent pole.

FINDING INFORMATION

The information you need varies drastically, depending on, among other things, where you are going and for how long, whether you plan to follow a well-established trail or head out into the great unknown, and whether you're staying close to home or venturing to a different part of the country (or a different country altogether). At a minimum, you'll need to know what kind of weather to expect, the trail conditions, and predictable difficulties you may encounter. How do you find out whether the trail has been washed out by last year's floods? Whether camp-spoiled freeze-dried food–loving bears still infest a favorite area? Or whether the season's late snowmelt makes stream crossings dangerous?

Local outfitters. Before you start putting miles on your boots, let your fingers do a little walking for you. Look in the yellow pages under "outfitters," "sporting goods," or "camping supplies." Call the store and ask if they have guidebooks. If the answer is yes, they probably have a lot more information, including maps, how-to books, sales clerks who know the areas, and maybe even a bulletin board where local hiking clubs post notices of upcoming events.

Hiking clubs. Whether they are huge, sophisticated organizations with paid staffs and publications or small, ad-hoc groups whose activities are limited to maintaining a few miles of a local trail, hiking clubs can be your best source of information, including weather, arrangements for car shuttles, water availability, trail conditions, recommended guidebooks, trailhead parking, public transportation, and services available in towns near the trail. To find out about hiking clubs, start with the American Hiking Society (P.O. Box 20160, Washington, DC 20041; 301-565-6704), which maintains a list of member clubs and organizations. Officers of the club may be able to answer your questions—or they may direct you to other members who lead the kind of trip you're planning to take.

Regional hiking guides. Guidebooks often contain important seasonal information about temperature, precipitation, water sources, insects, and trail conditions. But what if you live in New York and you want to plan a trip to California? Try a mail-order outlet like the Adventurous Traveler Bookstore (800-282-3963) catalog. Also check out *Books in Print* (available at libraries), which indexes books by subject, author, and title. Once you know a book is in print, you can request it through the interlibrary loan program.

Maps. A good (and cheap) source of regional information is the USDA Forest Service. Each national forest sells its own 1:125,000-scale map, and many of these maps include information about trail conditions, weather patterns, and dangerous plants and animals.

On-line information. Trail organizations and individual hikers share information through home pages on the World Wide Web and through hiker bulletin boards. Two places to try are *BACKPACKER* magazine at AOL (http://www. bpbasecamp.com) and GORP on the World Wide Web (http://www. gorp.com), which have links to a variety of hiking clubs and resources.

The Internet is a useful tool for planning hikes and getting information about gear, techniques, and trail conditions. Visit *Backpacker's* website at http://www. bpbasecamp.com. (Photo: Jeff Scher ©ERG)

Land management personnel. Try ranger stations for information about USDA Forest Service and National Park Service lands. Ask to speak with someone who has firsthand information about the trails you're planning to hike.

KEEPING GEAR LIGHTWEIGHT AND ESSENTIAL

There's no such thing as a perfect gear list. Over the course of dozens of backpacking trips, you might never go out with exactly the same things in your pack. Your favorite items wear out, new gear is developed to take their place. You don't need as many emergency extras for a 3-day trip as you do for a 10-day trip. Some trips involve vast swings in temperature. Some destinations require one water bottle; some require two. But no matter how different your destinations—no matter whether you're camping in Yellowstone in February or Arizona in September—a few constants apply. You want your pack to be as light as possible, and you want to carry exactly what you need, and not an ounce more.

▲ ▲ ▲

Make Your Own Trail

Here's a wonderful thing about backpacking: When it comes to where to go, there aren't any rules to follow. Starting with the information in guidebooks, you can create your own trail. By venturing off the guided path, you might find that, while some trails look like the backcountry equivalent of the interstate highway system, others are lonely from lack of use. There's still plenty of solitude in the backcountry. Here's how to find it:

- Almost all guidebooks tell you the names and addresses of the land management agency you'll be hiking through, so your first order of business is to get a map. A Forest Service map (1:125,000 scale) is fine.
- Using a highlighter, trace the route of the trail you intend to hike. (This might be the original guidebook trail that caught your attention.)
- Then check out other trails in the area. There might be opportunities to connect trails together and make a loop (really convenient for trailhead transportation and getting back to your car). Don't ignore little dead-end trails—many of them are infrequently used, and some of them go to spectacular campsites at isolated places where no one goes.
- Check with the land management agency regarding the trails' difficulty and condition. Also ask which maps they recommend you use. Sometimes, a 1:125,000-scale map is adequate for following a trail—but it tells you nothing about elevation. A 7½-minute map tells you everything you need to know—but you need a lot of them, because they don't cover big distances. A good compromise is a commercially produced 1:62,500-scale map, if one is available for the area you plan to hike in.
- Finally, you don't need a guidebook to figure out mileages; do it yourself with a map measuring device like a mileage

wheel. Careful: The result is likely to be a little short of accurate. If your wheel tells you the hike is 10 miles long, figure 11 or 12, because of all the zigs and zags and ups and downs that don't show up on a map.

How much can you carry? Aim for no more than one-fourth of your body weight to start, one-fifth of your body weight if you're out of shape and already hauling around a few extra pounds of your own. Very fit hikers can handle one-third of their body weight, and in some cases more. What does that translate to? A couple sharing equipment should be able to keep their pack weights under 40 pounds each. For average three-season hiking, 5 days' worth of food (about 10 pounds per person) is a comfortable load. If you're heading out for more than a week or so, you'll want to think about resupplying en route.

Keep a gear list. I made my generic three-season list the day I climbed Katahdin at the end of my Appalachian Trail through-hike. The highest mountain in Maine and the northern terminus of the Appalachian Trail, Katahdin offers classic three-season backpacking in early September (read: anything might happen), and I figure that anything I actually hauled the 2,000 miles of the Appalachian Trail, I really needed. Also, keeping a list means I'm less likely to forget all those little forgettables, like allergy medicine, a bandanna, or a clothesline. Many hiking guides (but not this one) contain suggested gear lists. You can start with them, but remember: Even the folks who wrote up those lists for you don't go out with the same stuff every single time. So think about what kind of trip you're taking in what kind of weather, and modify the list accordingly.

Cull one more time. After you make your list and check it twice, after you pile everything on the living room floor and then reject anything you don't absolutely need, go through your gear again. Do you really need all that moleskin? A whole bottle of aspirin? Two extra T-shirts?

Share gear. Do a gear dump with your hiking partners. You don't each need your own toilet trowel, stove, knife, cord, first-aid kit, roll of duct tape, spice kit, firestarter, and guidebook. Depending on the length of your trip, there might be other items you can share as well: small items, like sunscreen and bug dope. Or big (read: heavy) items like a tent. But before you marry your pot to your partner's stove, be sure you're committed to staying together for the length of the trip. And be sure—before one of you charges ahead or lags behind—that each of you has what is needed for the day's walk.

Useful units. Even if you intend to walk together at the same pace, make sure each of you has complete useful units: The person carrying the stove should have the pots and the fuel; the person with the tent gets the whole thing, including poles. The person with the stove should carry the ground cloth or space blanket; the person with the tent gets the food that can be eaten cold. That way, if you get separated by accident, you each have gear you can make use of.

Get rid of the unnecessary extras. Question everything. Just because a piece of equipment comes with something doesn't mean you have to lug it around. An example: Most internal-frame packs come with a "bonnet"—the compartment at the very top where you might stash your rain gear and a lunch. These compartments are usually removable for use as a day pack, but I never thought of leaving the compartment at home until a fellow hiker pointed out that for a midsummer hike in New York, the pack had plenty of capacity without those extra ounces. Another example: If your down jacket comes with a removable hood, consider whether the hike you're planning requires the hood *and* a hat *and* a balaclava, or just one of these. If your cook kit came with nesting pots and several utensils, consider how many pieces you actually need. If your pack has a crampon protector, consider whether you own, or ever intend to own, a pair of crampons. If the answer is no, get rid of those extra ounces.

The value of a trial run. Check out the fit of your pack when it's loaded down with actual gear (as opposed to those sandbags you used to try the pack on in the store). Put some real trail miles on your boots, and see how they feel when you bang your toes against a few rocks. Make sure your shorts don't ride up between your thighs, your shirt doesn't have seams exactly under your pack's shoulder straps, and everything that's supposed to fit inside your pack actually does.

Doing double duty. One of the best ways to lighten the gear load is to look for items that do double duty. An example: A water bag blown up with air like a balloon can be a pillow. So can a stuff sack filled with extra clothing.

Consolidate batteries. Try to choose battery-powered items that use the same type of batteries. For instance, many flashlights, cameras, and portable radio or tape players (if you bring them) use AA batteries. You'll save weight on spares, and you can take the battery out of your camera and use it as a spare for your flashlight.

Guidebooks. Some publishers print fancy guidebooks with color pictures—great for the coffee table, not so great for the campsite. Photocopy the relevant pages (reduce the size if necessary, so that you get two pages of the guidebook on one piece of paper; if you copy on both the front and back, you can cut the weight of your guidebook in half again) and leave the book at home. Cheaper guidebooks can simply be torn apart: If you're doing a 5-day hike on northern California's Pacific Crest Trail, there's no need to lug along information about the Mojave Desert. Pull out the section you're going to use and keep the pages in a resealable plastic bag. A guidebook page you're done with can be saved for reminiscence or reuse—or it can serve in an emergency as firestarter.

Maps. Trimming the edges off your maps makes them smaller and easier to line up with each other, but wait! Hold those scissors! Most map margins contain useful information, including declination, the names of adjoining maps, the scale, and the elevation between contour lines. Before you slash, make a note of relevant information you're cutting out. Similarly, use caution about trimming your maps down to your exact narrow route: if you get lost or need to find a shortcut out, you'll want to know about those side trails or that old logging road down in the valley.

PACKING TIPS

Keeping your gear straight. Stuff sacks are backpacking's answer to file cabinets. For a long time, manufacturers favored red and blue stuff sacks, which led to conversations like this:

"Hey, Karen! Pass the tent bag."

"Which one is that?"

"The red one."

"Which red one?"

"That one."

▲ ▲ ▲

The Ten Essentials

In the 1930s, The Mountaineers came up with a list for its climbing students. Over the years, the list became known as the Ten Essentials, although over time and through the opinions of writers of outdoor books like this one, some additions have snuck in. After all, there is a whole passel of conditions that require a whole lot more than just ten essentials.

This list errs on the side of more rather than less, retaining The Mountaineers' original list, but adding some extra items that are especially appropriate for backpackers and hikers. So yes, if you want to be technical about it, there are more than ten items. But if you've got the following equipment in your pack, chances are good that you'll be able to deal with the unexpected.

Some of these items are common sense; others enable you to deal with a variety of problems. Do you absolutely always need every single one of them? If you've hiked the trail before and know it well, or if you're on a midsummer day hike in the lowland temperate zone, maybe you can do without a compass or those extra clothes. But remember: Nature does have a habit of turning ornery just when you least expect it. Turn to the sidebars in the chapters indicated to find out what's so essential about these essentials.

Map (chapter 3)

Compass (chapter 3)

Extra clothing (chapter 6), including rain gear (chapter 6)

Firestarter (chapter 5)

Matches (chapter 5)

Sunglasses and sunscreen (chapter 6)

Extra food (chapter 2), including water and a way to purify it (chapter 8)

Pocket knife (chapter 5)

First-aid kit (chapter 7)

Flashlight (chapter 4)

▲ ▲ ▲

Things to Do with an Old Foam Pad

- Cut out a piece big enough to sit on during breaks.
- Wrap it around your water bottle as an insulator.
- If your pack is poking you, stick a piece of pad in the offending place.
- Use it as a stove pad in the winter.
- Wrap it with duct tape and use it as a cutting board.

"This one?"

"No, the other one!"

Fortunately, more colors have become available in recent years, and it's a good idea to mix 'em up. Go for bright colors: You won't end up leaving one behind by accident. (Don't worry—you're not violating low-impact courtesy—your stuff sacks spend most of their time hidden in your pack, right?)

Keeping equipment dry. If you're buying new equipment or upgrading, go for waterproof bags. Nothing you haul around in your pack needs to be any wetter than necessary. But don't bother with expensive waterproof/breathable fabric like Gore-Tex (nothing in your pack is breathing, right?). Garbage bags will do in a pinch (they can also be used to line non-waterproof stuff sacks). Clear garbage bags let you see what's inside. Get heavy-duty ones.

Wrap an old foam pad around your water bottle as an insulator. (Photo: © Dorcas Miller)

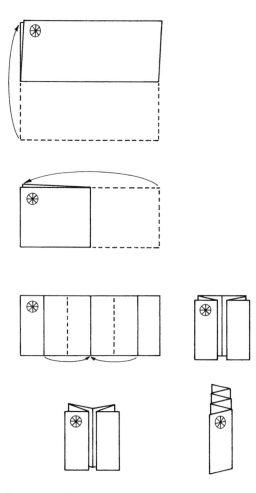

Figure 1. Folding a map into an accordion as shown will enable you to see any part of the map without having to unfold the whole thing.

Balancing your load. Experiment! The standard way to pack is for the heavy stuff to ride high up and close to your back. But if you're going off trail, try packing the heavier stuff a little lower than usual. You'll appreciate the better balance on tough terrain. Because of their generally lower center of gravity, women often prefer this method of packing—regardless of the terrain.

Packing for convenience. Carry your lunch and snacks where you can get at them without having to un- pack your stove, your fuel, and your extra clothing. Ditto for your toilet paper and trowel. Keep your rain gear and pack cover handy.

Maps. Folding a map as shown in Figure 1 makes it possible to see any part of it easily. Keep the day's map in a resealable plastic bag.

Where did I put the car keys? Pack car keys, money, credit cards, and your driver's license where you won't have to handle them. My pack has a handy little zippered compartment in the underside of the bonnet. Keys and money go there and remain untouched until I need them.

Useful extras. It is a real pain in the neck to have to take off your pack and put it back on every time you need a little something. A small pouch hanging from your waist belt, or a fanny pack worn backward, puts little necessities like sunscreen and bug dope at your fingertips.

Small containers. Film canisters make lightweight, water-resistant containers for soap, needles, safety pins, wood matches, and other small losable items. Don't use them for food or spices; they contain residue from photographic film. Those sample-sized bottles you get in hotels for shampoo are good for liquid soap, calamine lotion, and rubbing alcohol. You can also buy small plastic containers at an outfitting store.

Packing small items. Pack small items according to how and when you use them, not what they are. Logically, you wouldn't think that you should keep your toothbrush next to your tent pegs, but I brush my teeth when I'm in camp—so pegs and toothbrush live together in an "everyday ditty bag" that contains small daily necessities like my headlamp, notebook, and comb. The tent repair sleeve, the extra tent pole, the first-aid kit, and my extra batteries go in my "backup bag." Items can migrate from one bag to another. For instance, at the beginning of the trip, it's a good idea to keep your blister stuff where it's handy, but if you haven't gotten a blister after a couple of days, the moleskin can go into hiding in the backup bag.

How to find things in the dark. Pack consistently. Get in the habit of packing things in the same place every day. You'll spend less time rummaging around, and in an emergency you'll be much more efficient.

THINGS TO CHECK BEFORE YOU LEAVE HOME

Stove. Many liquid gas–fueled stoves, such as the popular MSRs, come in two parts: the stove assembly, which includes the burner that you cook on, and the pump unit that screws into your fuel bottle. You can leave the pump unit screwed into your fuel bottle for the duration of your trip, but beware: Check to make sure you've got both parts of your stove the next time you head out!

Fuel bottles. The stove manufacturers insist on making their own slightly differently threaded fuel bottles. If your stove uses the fuel bottle as part of the assembly, make sure that the bottle you take fits the stove you're going to use. (Same thing goes for when you buy a fuel bottle.)

▲ ▲ ▲

Weighing In

We've all hefted our packs and asked just exactly what it is that weighs so much. Below, I've put pounds and ounces to some of the major gear I carry on a three-season hike. This is the bare-bones list—no fancy extras—for a 5-day trip. Because I, like many hikers, usually travel with a partner, I separated out the communal gear. If you're going solo, you've got to haul all of it yourself—another reason to find a partner.

Personal Gear

Backpack: 7 pounds
20-degree sleeping bag: 3½ pounds
Rain gear (pants, jacket, pack cover): 2 pounds
Bag of clothing (one change of hiking clothes; extra layers, camp shoes): 3 pounds
Sleeping pad: 2 pounds
Miscellaneous personal gear, including headlamp, journal, daily necessities, mosquito goop, sunscreen: 2 pounds
Total: 19½ pounds

Communal Gear

Tent for two, including stakes, ground cloth, poles: 5 pounds
Stove: 1 pound
Cook kit for two, including pots, dishes, utensils, cups, knife: 2 pounds
Fuel in fuel bottle: 2 pounds
First-aid kit (stripped down): ½ pound
Water filter: 1 pound
Guidebooks and maps: ½ pound
Total: 12 pounds

Consumables

Food (2 pounds per person per day): 10 pounds
Water (2 pounds per quart): 2 pounds
Total: 12 pounds

Grand Total: 37½ pounds if you're hiking with a partner; 43½ pounds if you're going solo.

Priming equipment. If you use a stove such as the Optimus that requires a dab of fuel to prime it, make sure you've got a tiny gas funnel, some priming paste, or an eyedropper (plastic, not glass). In a pinch, you can soak a cotton swab in white gas or alcohol, place it in the priming cup, and light up.

Tent poles. Make sure you have your tent poles: The right number of the right kind. Ditto for tent stakes.

Backpack waistband buckles. I admit, this sounds dumb. I got to the trailhead, jumped out of the car, swung on my pack, and reached for those plastic buckles to snap the waistband shut. And reached again. It took me three tries to realize the buckle wasn't there: I'd swiped it to use on another pack and forgotten to replace it.

Bootlaces. Bootlaces sometimes get removed when boots are cleaned and treated. Make sure you've put them back. The same for boot innersoles.

▲ ▲ ▲

Don't Leave Home without It!

Okay, so I told you to pack light. But part of packing light is taking along things that can do more than one job. Like the following:

Bandanna. Use as a napkin, washcloth, headband, bandage, towel, pot grabber, hat, scarf, and prefilter for turbid water.

Duct tape. Among its uses: first aid for blisters, holding together delaminating boots, and a temporary patch for torn gear. (Waterproof athletic tape is another excellent fix-all.)

Walking sticks. Use these for propping up a tarp, supporting you in stream crossings, probing rocky ground for snakes, warding off farm dogs, pushing your bear-proof food bag up out of reach, flicking debris off the trail, and saving your knees on a steep descent.

Cord. Use for drying clothes, hanging bear bags, tying things onto your pack, lowering a water bottle into a hard-to-reach water source (see Figure 10), lowering a pack down a cliff that you can't descend with a pack on, and guying out your tent. Carry 40 feet of it.

Cheesecloth. Use as a prefilter, bandage, mosquito netting, or coffee filter.

Space blanket. Use for a makeshift shelter, ground cloth, emergency wrap, or tablecloth, or to protect your gear when you're making camp in the rain.

Dental floss. Useful for the obvious function, plus stitching and tying things together.

Garbage bags. Use as a pack cover. Sit on them on rainy days. Isolate your wet rain gear from dry gear in camp. Waterproof your sleeping bag. Wear as an emergency rain jacket or windbreaker.

Elastic cords. Use for holding miscellaneous items onto your pack or holding broken things together.

Whistle. This carries farther than a shout, although generally not as far as you wish it would.

Baking soda. Use for toothpaste, boot deodorizer, foot soak, and deodorant.

Closed-cell foam pad. Don't throw out your old one! Cut it into pieces and use it to pad your ice-ax handle (which makes it more comfortable to use as a walking stick). For other ideas on its usefulness, see the sidebar Things to Do with an Old Foam Pad, in this chapter.

Repair kit. See chapter 9, Field Repairs.

Insect repellent. You know why.

TRAVEL TIPS

Trailhead parking lots. Driving to the trailhead may be troublefree transport, but leaving your car in a trailhead parking lot can be another story altogether. Even a tired old beater can become the target for thieves and vandals—especially if you're parking an out-of-state car in rural communities where there is a schism between the local folks and the tourists. Call the local hiking club to find out whether there have been reports of vandalism at the trailhead (and specify if you have out-of-state plates). If you do leave your car at a trailhead lot, park so that the car is visible from the road, and don't leave anything—not even a ratty old pair of jeans, and certainly not an expensive radio—in sight inside the car.

Trailhead parking alternatives. Ask local business owners near the trail (best bets: gas stations, stores, hotels, and restaurants) if you can park your car in their lot. From there, you can hitch to the trailhead or offer to pay someone to drive you. Another option: Local hiking clubs have lists of people who are available to shuttle. You can pay them to drive you to the trailhead, keep your car for you, and pick you up when you're done with your hike.

Walk in circles. Loop hikes, where you hike out on one trail and return on another, are a great way to avoid having to pay someone to shuttle you a long distance. You can make your own loop by linking together existing trails on local forest service, Bureau of Land Management, or park service maps. But agency maps can be out of date, so call the ranger station or agency responsible for managing the trail and make sure that all the segments of your loop still exist.

Car keys. Tape an extra one under your car somewhere where you have to get really dirty and swear a lot to find it again.

Protect your pack. When traveling by plane to the hiking area, use duffel bags to protect your backpack. Buy a humongous inexpensive duffel that will hold your pack and all the extras (telescoping hiking sticks, air mattress, hiking boots). Then pick up an unassembled (i.e., flat) cardboard shipping box at your local post office and cram it into the duffel, along with some mailing tape and an address label. When you get to your destination, keep your backpack with you for your hike and, rather than lugging the duffel on your hike, send it to yourself in care of a hotel where you will stay at the end of your trip. If you don't plan on using a hotel, you can send the duffel to yourself in care of general delivery to a post office. Then, at the end of your hike, you can repack your backpack in the duffel for the flight home.

Baggage handler – proofing the naked pack. Take off the waistband, or at the very least buckle it tightly around the pack. Tighten and tie all hanging straps as securely as possible. Wrap the whole thing in garbage bags and secure with a ton of duct tape, then tie the package up with rope, which the baggage handlers can (presumably) use to toss your pack around.

No stove fuel on planes. It's against the law to put anything flammable in your luggage and, of course, that includes stove fuel, both liquid fuel like white gas and butane cartridges. If your backpacking jaunts are such that you start racking up frequent flyer miles, you should have a multifuel stove, which runs on (among other things) unleaded gasoline, kerosene, white spirits, dry cleaning fluid, and aviation fuel.

Protect your pack. You never know how it will be handled, so make it travel-proof by stowing gear inside the pack and securely attaching any add-ons. (Photo: Jeff Scher ©ERG)

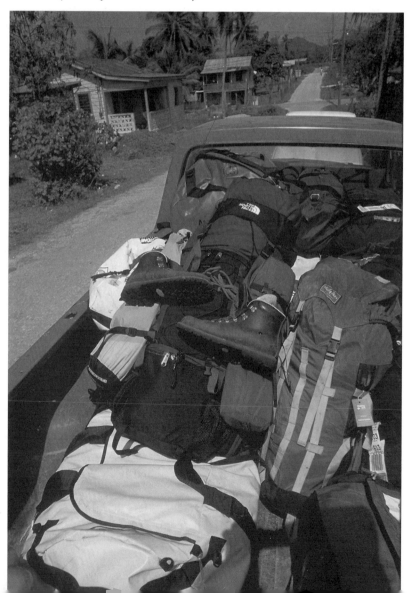

But a warning: Don't count on anything working in the field that you haven't first tried at home!

Burn off extra fuel. No stove fuel on planes means no fuel, period. Burn off any excess that might be lurking in your stove's tank or gas lines.

Check with the airlines. Some airlines refuse to transport camping stoves, fuel or no fuel. It's better to check before you go. These rules are arbitrary and differ from airline to airline, so before you make your plane reservation, be sure the airline accepts stoves.

Preventing spills. The change in air pressure in the baggage compartment of a plane can also cause explosions of a less flammable nature. Anything liquid or sticky or goopy belongs in a sealed plastic bag. Make that two sealed bags. This is also true if you're going to be climbing: A change of as little as 4,000 or 5,000 feet can pop the top off of your medications, lotions, mosquito repellent, or margarine and leave you with a gooey mess inside your pack. Be especially vigilant if you pack your bags at sea level, fly to a higher altitude such as the Rockies, and head uphill.

Lost luggage blues. Make sure you've got at least an hour between connecting flights, more in the winter if you're going through northern cities that are prime targets for the meteorologist's revenge. It does absolutely no good to put your real address and phone number on your luggage tags if you're headed somewhere else and no one is at home to take a call from the airline. You do need to write down your real address on the tag—just in case your pack travels to China without you and it takes months to get it back. But also be sure to write down your destination and a local contact. (If you don't have one, try the local forest service office or hiking club.) Never check valuables (like cameras), essentials (like medicines), or irreplaceable items (like the maps on which you spent several hours drawing your route).

Oversized luggage. Oversized luggage might be loaded or unloaded separately, or it might even be shipped with cargo, where it is subject to even more abuses. Caution: If you find your backpack treated as oversized luggage, you might want to reevaluate your definition of the word "essential." Check and make sure that you really do need to haul all that stuff with you.

Locking up. Teeny locks on luggage zippers do nothing to keep out determined thieves, but they do deter sticky fingers from taking a tour through your stuff. Combination locks mean that you'll have one less key to lose. If you don't have a lock, twist a garbage tie through the zippers; anything you can do to delay a thief deters a thief.

Weight limits. On international flights, check luggage weight limits going to *and* from your destination. On some international carriers, you're permitted 150 pounds going, but only 44 pounds returning. (Go figure!) For a returning backpacker, 44 pounds is plenty, but if you're trucking along a suitcase of city clothes and next year's Christmas presents, you could go over the limit.

PLANNING FOR SAFETY

Your itinerary. Leave a copy with a friend. Choose someone who is at least marginally familiar with the vocabulary of backpacking, and tell this person the trails you intend to hike and—if you know—approximately where you expect to camp. Make sure your friend knows when you're expected to come out of the woods.

Trailhead registers. Sign in whenever possible; in an emergency it helps land management personnel locate you. If possible, share your itinerary with local land management personnel—along with an emergency contact.

Check into rescue costs and insurance. This is especially important when traveling abroad or in Canada, where rescue policies differ from those in the United States. Local rules may require you to register or to buy insurance or a camping permit. If you need to be rescued and haven't followed local protocol, you could be in for one whopping helicopter bill.

Don't share your plans with strangers. Trail chitchat about where you came from and where you're going is harmless, but people you meet on the trail or in trail towns don't need to know where you intend to sleep. Set up your camp out of sight of the trail; it's good low-impact manners, and it's safer if you can't be seen by anyone who happens along.

Hunting season. It's disconcerting to top a ridge and see a hunter sheepishly trying to pretend that he was really aiming at something

Registering at the trailhead helps rangers find you if there is an emergency. (Photo: ©Karen Berger/Daniel R. Smith)

else as you came over the rise. Hunting season varies by state, animal, and even method of killing. (Some states have powder, bow hunting, and regular seasons on deer alone, and then there's grouse, turkey, elk, moose, and bear.) Be aware of the season, and ask locally about areas that are off limits to hunters, or not frequented by them.

Wear hunter orange. Forget about fitting in with the environment; during hunting season, aim to look like a fluorescent pumpkin. Go for orange front, back, and top: that means a hat, a vest, and a pack cover. (The Appalachian Trail Conference sells a reversible pack cover that is colored hunter orange on one side.)

Leave the roads behind. Most hunters don't stray too far from roads because they don't want to have to go a long way to carry out their kill. Choose places to hike that aren't close to roads.

Avoid hiking alone. If you do hike alone, the above cautions go double.

RESUPPLYING ON THE TRAIL

On long trips—say, more than a week—you'll need to resupply en route. You can look on a map to find towns near the trail, and plan to buy food as you go. This strategy requires the least preparation and it gives you more flexibility to change your plans. The downside is that you'll be stuck with the offerings of a small-town grocery store; if some other hiker just bought the last jar of peanut butter, you could be out of luck. Also, you're limited to buying whatever package sizes are available: a four-pack of soup when you only need two; a whole family-sized box of instant potatoes when maybe you're not quite *that* hungry. If you're picky about your food, you might not appreciate the white bread, processed cheese, sugared cereals, and preservative-filled lunch meats that are staples of small-town stores. The smaller the town, the more difficult you'll find resupplying on the fly.

Food drops. One popular option, used by most long-distance hikers, is to send yourself a "food drop" (or, if you're traveling for an extended period of time, coerce a loving friend into sending your boxes for you). Pack a box of supplies you'll need and address it as follows, including your expected arrival date:

Your name
c/o General Delivery
Town, State, zip
Please hold for hiker arriving on or about (date)

General delivery holds packages for 10 days. Make sure you put a return address on the box in case your plans change. Check with your local postmaster to find out which is the cheapest way to send your package; over long distances, priority mail often costs about the same as parcel post, and it gets your package where it's going much faster.

Remember, private delivery services like UPS cannot deliver to a general delivery address or a post office box.

Commercial establishments. Some commercial establishments near major trails will hold hiker packages. You'll usually find information about these places in guidebooks about the specific trail. Check first to make sure the business is still accepting packages. Ask if they charge and how much (most don't charge a fee, but in very remote areas, there may be a small charge, either by the box or by the day) and if they have any packing requirements. Hint: Proprietors will be more willing to help you if you indicate that you plan to patronize their business when you're in the area!

On a long trip, you might need to resupply en route. (Photo: ©Karen Berger/Daniel R. Smith)

Deliver your own mail. Another way to resupply is to hand deliver the items yourself before your hike. Some ranger stations, restaurants, or shops near the trail will hold packages. Always call first, and be sure you know their hours and days of operation.

▲ ▲ ▲

The Soloist

You probably already know all the reasons not to hike alone: You make better decisions with a partner. There is safety in numbers (there has never, for example, been a documented case of a grizzly bear attacking a party of four people or more). Your partner might recognize a danger you blithely pass by. Another hiker might have a piece of gear you forgot or didn't realize you'd need, or a skill. And if one of you falls or is injured, there's someone to go for help.

Nonetheless, many hikers take those risks because they can't find a compatible partner or because they like the experience of being alone in the wilds. If you do head out solo, here are some things you should do in addition to the rest of the advice in this chapter:

- Stick with your original plans—both your route and your schedule. If something goes wrong, rescue workers will know where to look.
- Don't take unnecessary risks. Go around the ice chute instead of across it. Take the extra half hour to find a really safe way across that snowmelt stream.
- Pay attention. Even a little mishap like tripping and spraining your ankle can have serious repercussions for a solo hiker.
- Carry a signaling device: A whistle, a flashlight, or a mirror can make it easier for rescuers to find you.

Little things to make your life easier. In addition to food, your resupply drops can contain premeasured quantities of consumables you need on the trail, like boot goop, toothpaste, spices, vitamins, small sample-sized bottles of shampoo and soap, a resealable plastic bag of laundry detergent, personal supplies, sunscreen, bug dope, journals, map and guidebook pages for the next leg of your trip, a book, film, new matches, an extra pair of socks, and toilet paper. Many of these items are difficult to purchase in remote towns, and even when they are available, they might not be exactly what you're looking for or you may have to buy a larger quantity than you need.

Sending back the overload. Unless you're a genius at packing for the trail, chances are you'll have a few things in your pack you don't need. Maybe you misjudged the weather and you just don't need that extra sweater. Or you've used up half of your guidebook, but want to keep it for a repeat visit. Include a mailing label, some tape, and a large padded envelope in the resupply box to send home extras like spare gear, spent film, and used maps. If you've really overpacked, you can buy shipping boxes at most post offices, but the clerks may or may not make mailing tape and address labels available.

CHAPTER 2

FOOD AS FUEL

▬

Planning Menus to Stoke Your Stomach

THE PERFECT DAY—weather, 65 degrees: cool enough to climb comfortably, warm enough to lounge about—and perfect terrain: challenging but doable; your muscles are luxuriating in that nirvana between use and abuse. You've done some work, and now it's payback time.

Dinner!

Backcountry cooks tend to fall into two categories. First, the just-add-water-and-mix crowd, figure backpacking is adventure enough without adding culinary daredevilry to their itinerary. They have a point: In bad weather, or when that last big climb was tougher than you are, who wants to be messing around with sautéing this and parboiling that?

Then there are the backcountry gourmets, the folks who turn up their noses at tuna-noodle supreme and spaghetti-plus-something. These are the people who find room in their packs for fresh vegetables and a fully stocked spice kit, and who might have sprouts growing out of their water bottles so they can whip up a backpack-grown salad. They too have a point: Just put one of their gourmet masterpieces next to one of the quick-and-easy concoctions and ask yourself which one you'd rather eat.

No matter which category you're in, you'll have to deal with the special demands of backcountry cuisine: The food has to be compact, resist spoiling, weigh as little as possible, and withstand sometimes extreme variations in temperature and humidity. And, whether your culinary creations are simple or complex, you'll most likely have to limit your wizardry to one pot and one stove.

Each backpacker ultimately strikes his or her own balance between convenience and creativity. What works on one trip might be entirely the wrong idea for another. A new continent, a particularly small small-town grocery store, or an unbelievably fussy hiking partner may all lead you to new, unfamiliar, and maybe even delicious culinary paths.

MENU PLANNING

To a great extent, your food planning is a function of what kind of hike you are on. How many days you're out limits your flexibility: On a weekend hike, you might have room in your pack for extras like a BakePacker (a contraption for wilderness baking) or a couple of pounds of fresh ingredients. A 10-day wilderness expedition, on the other hand, means that priority goes to lightweight foods that don't take up much space. In sunny weather, you might enjoy fiddling with complicated recipes, but if you've put in 20 miles in a driving rain, all you'll want to do is boil and eat.

How much is enough? You're the best judge of your own metabolism, but for starters, figure on carrying about 2 pounds of food per person per day for three-season hiking, and 2½ pounds for winter (you use up calories just staying warm). This assumes that the bulk of your food is quick-cooking, dried, or freeze-dried: in other words, lots of pasta, rice, cereals, et cetera. If you're packing in a supply of cans and fresh foods, you'll have to carry more weight to get the same number of calories.

Consult the meteorologist. The worse the weather conditions, the simpler your food preparation should be. You don't want to be messing around with lots of courses that need to be prepared just so when the sky is turning that weird shade of purple and the boomers are starting to roll. No matter what you think about freeze-dried meals, it's a good idea to pack one along: In truly horrendous conditions, it's going to be all you can do to boil a pot of water.

Test-drive new recipes. Be creative, but before you head outside, make sure your invention is edible. Check the quantities too, remembering that you'll be hungrier after toting a pack up and down mountains all day.

Plan treats. Throw in a treat per day. A tiny tin of oysters or anchovies can lift spirits at lunchtime on a rainy day, and an after-dinner chocolate bar will put you on the path to sweet dreams.

Read directions and ingredients. Some boxes of prepackaged food feature attractive pictures of veritable feasts. But you don't want to get into the backcountry and learn that the delicious-looking picture of noodles, meats, and vegetables assumes that you are providing the meats and vegetables. Also check cooking times and such required additional ingredients as oils or margarine.

▲ ▲ ▲

Essential Item: Extra Food

Why do you need it? Delays due to the unexpected: a lengthy detour, getting lost, an injury to you or someone in your party, a hike that turns out to be a lot harder and longer than you thought it would. There are any number of reasons why you might be out longer than you planned. A sackful of extra food does wonders to keep both your energy and your morale up.

How much? On a day hike, you can simply plan to tuck a little more than you think you'll need into your rucksack (such as a piece of fruit). On a backpacking trip, throw in a spare meal, a couple of extra instant soups, and a handful of spare snacks. Try GORP, but why stop there? Go ahead and add a few extras: some chunks of dried fruit, coconut chips, and a few handfuls of M&Ms. Candy bars are good instant energy boosts, as are any of a variety of different kinds of energy bars.

NUTRITION

Before you go. Worrying about nutrition the day before your hiking trip is a little like starting to train for a marathon the night before the race. What counts is what you've been doing regularly. Healthy people make healthy hikers.

Eat often. On short hikes, what you eat isn't nearly as important as how much you eat, and the right answer is "as often as you can." When you're tired, stop and eat. If your pack is too heavy, stop and eat. If you're getting cold, stop and eat. Get the picture? The calories are practically flowing out of you; put them back in throughout the day. Snack. Keep a resealable bag full of nuts or trail mix and a couple of cereal bars handy. Hint: Snacks high in complex carbohydrates, like dried fruit, cereal bars, and crackers, provide a quicker energy boost than high-fat foods. And they're longer-lasting than sugary snacks.

▲ ▲ ▲

Counting Calories

How many calories you burn is a function of your metabolism, your body weight, your fitness, the miles you hike, the elevation at which you're hiking, and how much weight you're hauling around in your pack. Appalachian Trail through-hikers are perhaps the most studied batch of backpackers, and the consensus seems to be that they use between 4,000 and 6,000 calories per day. How much, exactly, is 6,000 calories?

28 Kaiser rolls

3⅗ pounds of pasta

3⅘ 1-pound boxes of shredded wheat

12 5-ounce boxes of crackers

2½ pounds of almonds

What this means is that hikers tend to be a hungry lot, because very few of them can carry 6,000 calories for each day they're hiking. Even if they did, all that extra food would mean their packs would be even heavier, therefore requiring more calories to carry them. This vicious cycle means that backpacking is the diet secret of the ages: Eat as much as you can carry, walk all day, and watch the pounds melt off!

Vitamins. You don't need to worry too much about vitamin deficiencies on shorter hikes. If you're out for a weekend, bring along foods you like and eat as much as you want. On longer trips, consider supplementing your diet with vitamins or vitamin-rich foods, because the lightweight meals favored by backpackers tend to be deficient in some areas. A few suggestions: Brewer's yeast is a source of vitamin B. Wheat germ is a source of protein, thiamin, and vitamin E. Dried apricots contain vitamin A. Powdered milk has calcium. Whole grain cereals, crackers, and breads are good sources for B-complex vitamins.

STAPLES

Freeze-dried foods. Carefully read directions for freeze-dried meals. Freeze-dried is not necessarily synonymous with just-add-water. A hearty chicken and dumplings stew that gets good reviews for flavor but requires several preparation steps is not a good choice for a cold, rainy evening. The keyword for a lousy day is "no cook." Also double-check portion sizes. If you're out for an easy weekend, a freeze-dried dinner that says "two servings" may be enough for two people—especially if you take along an instant soup for an appetizer and a dessert of some sort. But if you're out for more than a couple of days, you may want those two servings all for yourself.

Noodle soups. Perennial backpacker favorites, quick-cooking noodle soups are Asian specialties, so go to the source. Asian food stores have a thousand kinds of instant noodles. This is a great way to add variety to your diet. And for those interested in squeezing a few extra calories into their packs, some of the soups come with tiny packages of calorie-packed oils for flavor. Because the directions are sometimes in another language, check the nutrition information, which is always in English: If there's any significant fat content, there's a little packet of oil hiding inside.

Pastas. Small or fine pastas like couscous and angel hair spaghetti are quicker cookers than bigger, heftier noodles and, ounce for ounce, they give you about the same number of calories. Appetites vary, but ¼ pound of pasta (plus sauce) is adequate for an average hiker, especially if you're packing some instant soup and maybe a dessert. Breaking spaghetti before you dump it in the pot makes it easier to eat with a spoon, the only utensil most backpackers carry.

Sauces. Try a can of tomato paste with a package of spaghetti-sauce spice mix, cheese sauce (maybe with a little ham, salami, or a can of chicken or tuna), or pesto sauce (packages are available, or dehy-

Backcountry staples include pasta, rice, and dehydrated fruit and vegetables. (Photo: ©Dorcas Miller)

drate your own). Note: Tomato sauce is also available in squeeze tubes; look for them in large supermarkets or specialty stores.

Rice. You're pretty much limited to quick-cooking rice in the backcountry because real rice takes too long (read: takes too much fuel), plus it's vulnerable to burning if you use one of those stoves where simmering is more difficult than it should be. Instant rice is good for hikes where water is a problem—in a desert, where water is scarce, or in winter, when you have to melt snow—because it takes less water to cook rice than it does to cook pasta.

Instant potatoes. What is true about rice is also true for instant potatoes. Try cooking them up with a can of ham and a package of mushroom gravy.

Prepackaged dinners. The noodle-and-sauce combinations by companies such as Lipton actually make convenient, lightweight hiker dinners. (One package intended to make four servings of a side dish is the right amount for one hiker dinner.) You can spice them up by adding Parmesan cheese, sun-dried tomatoes, dried mushrooms, Louisiana hot sauce, or dehydrated meat and veggies.

Canned foods. Take along a couple of small cans. A can of tuna, chicken, or ham can be added to lots of pasta combinations, giving you a protein boost and some additional flavor.

Snacks. Go for it! For hikers, snacks are a food group—and maybe the most important one of all. Your choice of snacks is limited only by your nutritional preferences and your taste buds. Candy bars are perennial favorites, but some hikers find that they need something with a bit more staying power. Energy bars (specially made for endurance athletes) are available at outfitting stores. Or you can make your own treats: Custom-design some GORP (Good Old Raisins and Peanuts) from your choice of raisins, nuts, dried fruit bits, chocolate chunks, M&Ms, and coconut slivers. Fruit breads like banana bread last well, and some hikers swear by fruitcake: That dense, calorie-packed, indestructibly tough-as-nails Christmas classic has all of the qualities of tailor-made hiking food!

▲ ▲ ▲

Honor Roll of Backcountry Favorites

Macaroni and cheese

Asian noodle soups

Spaghetti

Cheese and crackers

Peanut butter and pita

Instant oatmeal

Stuffing mix

Packaged noodle-and-sauce side dishes

Instant potatoes

Granola cereals

GORP

Healthy edibles. Your health food store is another source of food for the trail. Buying bulk lets you get the precise quantities you need, and unbleached, unprocessed foods provide better nutritional value. Health food stores also offer a selection of just-add-water dried foods like hummus, tabouli, and bean dip, which are both nutritious and easy to prepare.

Exotics. Do yourself a favor, and do your experimenting at home—at least to start. You may not have tasted freeze-dried foods, specialty store products, or favorites recommended to you by other hikers, and you don't want to find yourself staring down something you just plain don't like after a long day of hiking. Mix and match new flavors with tried-and-true favorites so you don't tire of either one.

FRESH FOODS THAT TRAVEL

To earn a place in your pack, foods have to be fairly light and resistant to spoilage. Hence the proliferation of quick-cook meals, dried foods, pasta, and grains in the backcountry kitchen. Fresh foods can't be the mainstay of your backpacking diet—they're just too heavy—but they can add a burst of flavor. Here are some that will last.

Salami, pepperoni, and sausage. Yes, the plastic-wrapped preservative-filled variety will last longer, but a slab from a German or Italian deli will hold up just fine for a few days and tastes even better.

Cheese. Cheese can survive for days without refrigeration. Hard cheeses last better than soft, so stay away from creamy Camemberts or Bries, and instead choose cheeses like Goudas, Edams, Cheddars, Jarlsbergs, and Swiss. Extra-sharp cheeses tend to be oilier, which can be messy in hot weather. Seal cheese in a double layer of resealable plastic bags, and on hot days, try to keep it in the middle of your pack.

Fruit. Apples last for several days. So do oranges; yes, they're heavy and you have to pack out the peels, but nothing tastes better at the top of a big climb.

Pita and bagels. These are better than regular bread, which squishes and crumbles in your pack. Breads with preservatives last longer, especially in humid climates. Choose denser, harder breads over light puffy loaves. Crackers don't spoil, but keep them in their cardboard boxes so they don't turn into crumbs.

Veggies. Root vegetables like carrots, onions, turnips, parsnips, and potatoes last well, but they take a while to cook, so think about fuel. Cauliflower and cabbage (but not broccoli) also survive well. Fresh garlic spices up just about anything. You can cook a potato by wrapping it in aluminum foil and throwing it in a low fire.

Smoked meats and fish. Bacon, sausage, ham, smoked salmon, and herring are great treats, but keep them out of bear country and be sure to hang them out of the reach of critters at night. These fine-smelling offerings attract unwelcome dinner guests from miles around.

Eggs. Yes, really. Hard-boiled eggs last several days—but so do eggs that have been dunked into boiling water for a minute or two, just long enough to cook the outermost millimeters of egg white, which makes the shell tougher. Still, be careful. If you're serious about your morning omelets, check out the egg carriers available at some outfitting stores. Or you can wrap the eggs in paper towels and put them in a tight-fitting container. Two choices that fit well inside a backpack: the cardboard tubes that Pringles potato chips come in, or the tubes you buy tennis balls in.

Butter. No need to go without. While fresh butter goes runny and rancid, clarified butter travels like a trooper. It's available commercially packaged for backpacking in convenient portion-sized plastic packets. Check your local outfitter or one of the mail-order trail food distribution companies.

A garden in your pack. You can grow your own sprouts. You'll need a water bottle, some cheesecloth, rubber bands, and sprouting seeds. Aside from that, all the seeds need in order to sprout is to be soaked in some water (treated, of course), drained, and then rinsed a couple of times a day. Specific directions depend on the kind of seed—as does sprouting time, which can take from 1 to 6 days. Obviously, quick sprouters (like mustard seeds, sunflower seeds, and wheat) are better choices for backpackers.

DEHYDRATING

Dehydrating food does several things that make sense for backpackers. It removes water, which makes food less susceptible to spoilage, and it lightens weight (and reduces bulk) while retaining flavor. In addition it's cheap and easy, and it provides superior nutritional value with no preservatives or chemicals.

In a pinch, you can dehydrate food in an oven set to its lowest temperature (usually 150 to 180 degrees), but best results require not only heat but air flow, and for that, a real food dehydrator is best. You can construct your own, but dehydrators are reasonably priced and widely available; check out health food stores, outfitters, and some department stores.

If you think jerky when you think dehydrated food, think again: Dehydrating aficionados say that if you can cook it, you can dry it—and that includes sauces, chili, thick soups, ground meats, and puréed fruit. The process is simple: Spread the foods evenly on a drying rack (don't crowd them together) and let them sit there until they look and feel right. Dehydrators come with directions that'll give you approximate drying times and help you get the hang of it.

Meats. Jerky makes a great trail snack. Slice the meat into even strips or cubes (about ¼ to ½ inch by 1 inch is good; the thicker the cut, the longer it will take to dehydrate). Cut away any excess fat, marinate in your favorite sauce (try soy sauce or teriyaki with fresh ginger and fresh-ground pepper), then dehydrate until the meat is the consistency of leather. You can also dehydrate ground cooked meats, which can then be added to sauces and stews. Dry fish till they are very hard if you plan to store them for long periods of time.

Dehydrating fruits or vegetables at home is easy, and the results are tasty additions to trail diets. (Photo: ©Alan Kesselheim)

Canned foods. By dehydrating canned foods like tuna and chicken, you can eliminate the weight of cans. An example: tomato sauce. Just spread it out and dehydrate until it becomes a strip of tomato-leather. Now you've got the food without the weight of the water—or the can.

Fruits. You can dehydrate raw fruit, or you can steam-blanch it first to cut down on spoilage. Steam for 3 to 6 minutes (longer for tough fruits like pineapples; shorter for soft fruits like peaches), then dunk into cold water. Wipe off excess water, then put into the dehydrator. For fruit leather, purée the fruit first, adding water until it is the consistency of applesauce. (Note: Some fruits such as berries don't require that you add water because they're juicy enough to begin with.) Then spread it evenly (about ½ inch thick) on a sheet of plastic wrap or parchment paper (not wax paper: it melts) and put it in the dehydrator. You can combine fruits, and even add raisins or nuts to vary the flavor and texture.

Vegetables. Virtually any vegetable can be dehydrated, including corn, tomatoes, onions, zucchini, and a host of other foods rarely seen on the trail. If you steam-blanch vegetables (to provide extra protection against spoilage), keep them in the dehydrator for a little longer than fruits. Dehydrated veggies can be added to virtually any meal. A great cold-weather snack: Mix a package of dried vegetables, a bouillon cube, and boiling water.

Sauces. Sauces, thick soups, stews, and chilis can all be dehydrated, the same way you dehydrate fruit leathers. After you've cooked up a batch, simply spread it out on plastic wrap or parchment and put the whole thing on a drying rack.

What not to dehydrate. Avoid dehydrating fatty foods, which can become rancid.

Strong-smelling foods. If you have a multirack dehydrator, don't dry foods with strong, spicy odors at the same time as other foods, or your strawberry fruit leather might end up redolent with the lingering essence of fish stew.

Drying tips. Small pieces dry faster than big pieces. If you're using plastic wrap, be sure not to cover the whole tray because you don't want to block air circulation. When you check foods, move them around a little and make sure there's room between pieces. If you're planning on storing the food for a long time before consuming it, dry it longer than foods to be eaten immediately. Thinner pieces (and thinner layers of sauces) dry harder than thick pieces. To speed up the process for sauces and fruit leathers, start by spreading them on a baking sheet and putting it in a slow oven instead of a dehydrator. Once they've reached a nonsticky state, peel them off the baking sheet and place the leather directly on the drying rack of the dehydrator to finish drying.

Storage. Keep dehydrated foods in brown paper bags to keep out light. The bag then goes in a plastic bag to help keep out moisture, then store it in a dark place. You can provide additional protection by putting the packages in a sealed glass or plastic jar. Write what's in each package so you don't mix up your strawberry purée with your tomato sauce. If you're getting into dehydrating in a big way, write the date on the label as well.

Reduce cooking time. In the field, different foods take different amounts of time to reconstitute. Presoaking can save both fuel and time. If you're eating something that takes a long time to rehydrate (beans, for example), add water to your meal at lunchtime (use a spare water bottle) and let the food rehydrate as you walk. Other foods can start rehydrating as soon as you arrive in camp. Use the leftover water to make soup; it contains nutrients from the reconstituted foods.

Precheck quantities. Dehydrated food does a bit of a disappearing act: When reconstituted, it doesn't seem to make as much—at least, that's how it seems to hungry hikers. So double-check quantities.

SPICING IT UP

Bouillon cubes. These are a terrific pick-me-up, especially on a day when you've worked hard and sweated harder. A couple of bouillon cubes can rescue a bland sauce or be mixed with hot water for a quick warm-up when you first get into camp.

Spice kits. Outdoor gourmets might go for one of the fancy (and weighty, considering their function) prefab spice kits available in outdoor stores. The rest of us can get by with freezer bags. Teeny little plastic bottles are better than resealable baggies for small quantities of spices because baggies gum up pretty quickly. Don't use film canisters; they contain traces of photographic chemicals.

Turn up the heat. If you like spicy foods, Louisiana hot sauce, Tabasco, or some exotic kind of cayenne pepper sauce makes everything taste better, including spaghetti, macaroni and cheese, and a whole slew of freeze-dried dinners. A little bit goes a long way, so repackage an ounce or two into a small plastic bottle.

Flavored oils. Spicy flavored oils are another way to add flavor and a few extra calories. A few drops of sesame or chili oil add zest to noodle soups. A dash of olive oil is good in spaghetti sauce.

Powdered sauces. Sauces are available to make chili, cheese sauce, spaghetti, and stroganoff, but if you're sensitive to MSG (monosodium glutamate) and preservatives, read the labels carefully. Check out your local health food store; their packaged foods almost certainly have fewer chemicals and preservatives—but they'll also be more expensive.

Gravy and soup mixes. You don't have to follow the directions; mixed with less than the suggested amount of water, soups and gravy mixes can be added to dried potatoes, rice, or pasta. If your concoction is too watery, use a little flour to thicken it.

▲ ▲ ▲

The Fix-everything Spice Kit

Onion flakes

Oregano

Garlic

Bouillon cubes

Cheese powder

Clarified butter

Parmesan cheese

Dried mushrooms

Sun-dried tomatoes

Bacon bits

Flour

Gravy mixes

Salt and pepper

Asian flavored oils like sesame and chili

Cayenne pepper sauce

Dried milk

Be a pack rat. Save up those little plastic packages of mustard, ketchup, barbecue sauce, and soy sauce you get when you order take-out food. In cool weather, you can even take along packets of mayonnaise. Just be sure you use the whole packet once it's opened. Mayonnaise starts to deteriorate as soon as it is exposed to air.

Miso. This Asian specialty comes in several types and flavors, but the standard is soybean-based and dark reddish brown. Add it to hot water for instant soup (it also comes dried in individual packets), or add it to a meal for flavor and added protein. It keeps well and is easy to pack in a resealable bag.

BEVERAGES

Water is the most important backcountry beverage, and drinking plenty of it might just be the most effective thing you can do to keep yourself healthy while hiking. It's so important that chapter 8 is devoted entirely to it. But for those who think variety is the spice of life, here are some other ideas.

Remember, however, that coffee, tea, and alcohol are diuretics, which means that they remove water from your system. If you do drink them, do so judiciously. Having recently returned from a 600-mile walk in the French and Spanish Pyrenees, I can with happy authority report that very little can start a hiker's day on a better note than a properly prepared bowl of *café con leche*. Ditto for ending it with a *flaçon* of red wine that goes down in the evening as smoothly as the setting sun.

Cowboy coffee. Camp coffee requires a pot and a way to heat it, period. Genuine java junkies all seem to have their favorite techniques, but the basic game plan is the same: Boil a pot of water, dump in the coffee, wait, and drink. Hint: To settle the grounds, tap on the side of the pot a couple of times before scooping out your dole; in winter, you can throw in a spoonful of ice. Dispose of the grounds by scattering them on the ground in an inconspicuous place.

Coffee bags. Single-portion coffee bags work on the same premise as tea bags—or, for that matter, a drip coffee filter. Water passes through the paper and extracts the coffee flavor. Some aficionados complain that bags make a watery brew, but coffee bags are certainly more flavorful than instant coffee (and easier to handle; they don't get gummed up in a resealable plastic bag). Tips: One bag makes one 8-ounce cup,

Some hikers carry along tiny trail espresso makers, but others prefer a small cone with filter. (Photo: ©Marypat Zitzer)

not a 12-ounce mug, and it needs to sit for several minutes to get reasonably strong. And keep the bags in the foil-lined containers for freshness. Yes, you'll have to pack out the annoying things, but if you're serious about your coffee, you'll appreciate the better taste.

Drip coffee. Let gravity do the work: Just bring along your favorite blend and one of those single-serving filter cones. Choose one with the thin metal mesh and you won't even have to worry about paper filters to pack out.

Tea. Tea bags are lightweight and simple to prepare, just like at home. Herbal teas contain no caffeine, are lightweight, and are a pleasant way to warm yourself up on a chilly night. Hot tea prepared at night becomes iced tea for the next day. And yes, pack out those tea bags.

Powdered artificially sweetened drinks. Drinks flavored with artificial sweeteners have no food value whatsoever, but they are extremely lightweight and mask the taste of iodine. If you like them, go ahead and pack them; they weigh next to nothing.

Powdered electrolyte replacement drinks. Stir-and-mix drinks like Gatorade have more food value (and, predictably, they are a lot heavier). If you're hiking in a desert, they can help prevent or treat dehydration. Each year, the rangers and medical workers in Grand Canyon National Park go through thousands of gallons of electrolyte replacement drinks, treating people who didn't listen to warnings about the sun and heat and what it does to you when you try to climb 5,000 feet.

Powdered fruit drinks. Powdered apple ciders and other fruit ciders are available (check your health food store). They help satisfy backcountry cravings for something that tastes like fruit. Some people find that they cause loose bowels, so experiment with small quantities before you start chugging liter after liter.

Powdered hot chocolate. Drink it first thing in the morning, last thing before you go to bed at night, or anytime in between when you need a hot drink. Hot cocoa has calories, sugar, and heat, and nothing tastes better on a cold blustery day.

Wine. No glass bottles, sorry (see the next section). If you do take wine, repack it in a plastic water bottle or a traditional leather wineskin. Oenophiles might turn up their noses at the plastic water bottle option, but it does allow you to chill that Chablis in a cold mountain stream.

PACKING AND PACKAGING

Invest in resealable plastic bags. Heavy-duty freezer bags do more to keep your stomach happy than any other piece of gear you carry. You can't take too many of these. They protect your food from moisture, spills, spoilage, and general grunginess. Everything goes in a resealable bag.

Cut down on garbage. Repackage food to get rid of bulk and weight. Count out quantities at home and put the major ingredients for each meal together. Cut out any directions on the package (you need to know how much water to add to the Stove Top Stuffing so you don't end up with Stove Top soup), and put them in the baggie with the food. Label the baggies clearly; in a tent in the dark, dried milk looks a lot like Parmesan cheese.

Prevent spills. Package squishy, oily, wet stuff that has the potential to spill all over your brand-new tent into reusable plastic squeeze tubes. These work for peanut butter, tomato paste, margarine, and mustard. Buy the size of tubes you think you'll need, and don't fill

Cut down on garbage by repackaging everything in resealable plastic bags. (Photo: Jeff Scher © ERG)

them with what they can hold—fill them with what you expect to use! Just in case, put them in a resealable bag.

Storing powdered foods. Powdery foods like sugar, dried milk, and flour tend to get caught in the channels of the closure device on resealable bags, especially in wet weather. Double-bag them, squeeze the air out, and wrap a rubber band around the package. If the zipper lock opens, the rubber band will cut down on spillage.

Have a Tupperware party. Plastic Tupperware bowls (or their equivalent) are great for backcountry eating because they're lightweight, yet tough enough to withstand bumping, dropping, and frequent exposure to heat. If you pack along their lids, they can be used to reconstitute dehydrated foods during the day. Then you can use the rehydrating water for making soups. If you don't use a bowl for rehydrating, use your water bottle.

Glass containers. How many times a day do you drop your pack and sit on it? Glass shatters. If a glass container breaks, you'll loose its contents into your pack, wasting food and creating a mess. You'll also create a danger to yourself and those who follow because you'll never be able to pick up all the shards. Even if you do, you'll be stuck carrying them for the rest of your hike. And they will rip other things in your pack. Starting to sound like a bad idea, right? For these reasons, glass is actually illegal in some national parks, and it's ill advised anywhere in the backcountry. Especially avoid taking it into hot springs.

Rationing for the long haul. If you're going out for a long hike, take precautions so you don't run out of food mid-hike. Premeasure ingredients and pack meal by meal. (For example, if you expect ½ pound of spaghetti to last for 2 days, divide it into two equal packages, one for each day.) Then put the food into two or three small stuff sacks rather than one big one. Each stuff sack should contain all the food necessary for a certain number of days. This helps ensure that you don't sneak a little of tomorrow's food into today's meal.

FORAGING

Sure, Lewis and Clark did it, but the world was different then. Today, you can't count on finding wild foods in abundance just when and where you need them. And, face it, at the end of the day, you're going to want

Rationing for a long-distance hike involves prepacking boxes of food that you mail to yourself and pick up in towns along the way. (Photo: ©Karen Berger/Daniel R. Smith)

to eat your dinner—not catch it. Still, the woods are full of delicacies that can add flavor, not to mention a few calories and fresh veggies to your diet. Hikers out for long hauls often feel veggie-deprived, which may be one reason that after being out in the woods for a few days, hikers gravitate to all-you-can-eat salad bars once they're back in town.

A word of warning: Many edible foods look just like their nonedible or even poisonous counterparts. Before you put anything into your cook pot, be sure you can positively identify it. Use regional field guides and, if you're really going to pursue an interest in wild foods, take a class at your local nature center.

Low-impact tip: wild foods. Whatever your foraging favorites, don't take too many of them from one place. Use only what you need for a supplement to your packed-in food; don't try to make wild foods the bulk of your backpacking diet.

Know the rules. Foraging is forbidden in some sensitive environments, so before you start to dine, be sure it's permitted.

Seafood. If you're hiking along a beach, look to the sea! Mollusks, mussels, oysters, clams—dig for them. Check locally, however. Make sure that shellfish harvesting is permitted in the area where you're hiking. Be careful of polluted waters, and especially the "red tides" (algae blooms) that can infect shellfish and cause paralytic shellfish poisoning—not a malady to court anywhere, much less in the backcountry.

Fishing. Don't forget: You need a license for every state in which you're fishing. If you've never fished before, you might want to tie a lure and a hook on a piece of string and try your luck the next time you're by a lake clouded with the summer mosquito hatch. Or you can bring real fishing gear. The recipe is simple: Throw your catch in a pan with some oil or butter, or wrap in foil and bake in coals. Delicious.

Disposing of fish entrails. Fish entrails are natural parts of the ecosystem, but in highly used areas, no one wants to come across traces of your activities. Don't throw entrails back in the stream. Bury them if the area is heavily used; otherwise, scatter them. In bear country, be sure to catch, gut, cook, eat, and dispose of fish well away from your camp.

Berries. Huckleberries, blueberries, wild strawberries, thimbleberries, raspberries, blackberries. There are some trails where it's a minor miracle anybody hikes any miles at all during the middle of summer with all the berry patches to slow them down. Snack until your tongue is huckleberry-blue, or collect a water bottle full of berries, add sugar and let it sit till the next morning. Make pancakes. You

Gooseberries cooked with a little sugar make a great fruit sauce.
(Photo: Jeff Scher © ERG)

can figure out the rest. Warning: Do not linger in berry patches in grizzly bear country.

Ramps. These onionlike plants grow in the southern Appalachians, where they are a favorite cooking ingredient for locals. Real ramp-o-maniacs eat them raw, but the rest of us sauté them and add them to soups, stews, and sauces.

Fiddlehead ferns. These early spring favorites have a crisp, delicate flavor. They are edible only as early spring shoots, and even then, don't eat too many, because they contain traces of cyanide. Once they unfold, they're completely poisonous.

Wild carrots. You know what these are: Queen Anne's lace. Be certain you identify them clearly; there are several very poisonous look-alikes. Queen Anne's lace always has "hairy"-looking stems, in contrast to poisonous look-alikes.

Daylilies. These dramatic summer blooms are equally at home in a vase or a salad dish. If you feel funny eating the flowers themselves, try a bite of an unopened bud.

Dandelions. All parts of the plant are edible, from roots to flowers. Try boiled dandelion roots: After cleaning off the root hair, boil until tender but not mushy, then add butter, salt, and pepper. The very young greens, when the flower heads are still tight little buttons, make a delicious and nutritious salad green.

Mushrooms. You've all heard the stories about mushroom poisoning, and some of them are true. But it's also true that the woods are full of pounds of tasty flavor that you don't have to carry. The best way to learn is to start close to home.

Don't begin with the idea you're going to learn all about mushrooms; instead, try to learn about one or two local species from an expert. Check out your local nature center and make sure you have your mushrooms down cold. Know what they look like in all stages of growth, what species they could be confused with, and how to tell them apart. Vet your information source: You need an expert, not somebody who once picked mushrooms with grandma.

Once you're very sure that you can safely identify a species, try it for the first time while you're still safely at home (near a hospital). Even commonly edible species can cause allergic reactions in sensitive indi-

Wild onion, dandelion leaves, Indian yampa root, and other wild edibles can liven up a one-pot meal. (Photo: Jeff Scher © ERG)

viduals. The best rules of thumb are to try only a tablespoon of cooked mushroom the first time you're trying a species, to only try one species at a time, and to keep several uncooked specimens for identification should you experience symptoms of poisoning. Symptoms can range from mild indigestion to severe food poisoning (to liver and kidney failure if you've eaten a very poisonous mushroom). Wait for 24 hours before assuming that you have no allergic reactions to the species.

If you're lucky enough to find a species you're sure you can identify while you're hiking, cook them as you would fresh storebought mushrooms back home. The ingredients for a tasty mushroom soup are easy to pack along. Sauté the mushrooms in clarified butter; then add onion flakes (or ramps), water, powdered milk, flour to thicken, and salt and pepper to taste.

Use trekking poles to help you climb hills and to take the pressure off your knees on steep descents. (Photo: ©Jeff Scher)

CHAPTER 3

ON THE TRAIL

Prepped for Adventure

"WHO'D HAVE EVER thought walking could be so hard?"

I heard it on the Appalachian Trail down in Georgia, where each year some 2,000 people take the first steps of a 2,000-mile journey to Maine. Only about 200 succeed.

I've also heard it on shorter hikes. And I've felt it myself a few times, on stiff climbs and on days where the mileage seems to stretch like saltwater taffy.

Why?

Maybe because walking and backpacking aren't the same thing, a fact that even experienced hikers forget once in a while. It takes some time to get used to hauling 40 pounds up a mountain on uneven terrain. It takes a reasonable level of fitness.

It also takes a little bit of know-how. It's amazing how a few tricks up your sleeve can get you across a scary-looking stream or up one of those mountains where the summit seems to move ever-higher. With a little bit of know-how, you can cope with that icy slope or the slippery scree. All it takes to walk comfortably is a reasonably fit body, a little preparation, and a little technique—which is what this chapter is about.

Note: On a related topic, check out chapter 7, Healthy Hiker, for tips on preventing and treating blisters and other backcountry problems.

BEFORE YOU GO

Choosing a hike. In addition to having great views, uncrowded camp-sites, and a pristine environment, the ideal trail is one that you can hike comfortably. If you haven't done a lot of climbing, watch out for a hike that requires too much elevation gain. How much is too much depends on your level of fitness, but here's something to think about: The Empire State Building is a little more than 1,000 feet tall. How many times in one day do you think you can climb it? Many trails have climbs of 1,000, 2,000, or even 3,000 feet. Don't underestimate what it takes to walk that far uphill: It can be every bit as daunting as the prospect of running up the stairs of the Empire State Building. Almost all backcountry woes can be traced to one simple cause: Trying to go too far too fast too high too soon. Plan the mileage and elevation care-fully for your first few hikes. Be conservative—you can always add on.

Checking the elevation. You can figure out elevation gain using a profile map, consulting a guidebook, or counting the contour lines on a topographic map.

Ask locally. National parks and forests (and some state parks, too) have staffs of rangers who can answer questions about trail difficulty and conditions. Trails can change from year to year, especially if they're not often maintained. In some extreme (but not unusual) cases, trails that are mapped on U.S. Forest Service maps have actually ceased to exist! You need to do your own homework: Call the land management agency to find out whether the trail you're thinking of hiking matches your level of fitness and experience.

UPS AND DOWNS

Hike at your own pace. Sounds simple, right? Just wait till you try it while your faster (or slower) hiking partner is pestering you to speed up (or slow down)! Avoid frustration by talking about mileage and pace before you head out. A couple of solutions: The faster person can slow down, go on ahead and wait at an agreed-upon spot, or take some pack weight to help the slower partner out.

Learn what your body can do. Your more experienced hiking partner may be the most well-meaning person in the world, but you can't trust someone else to know what your body is comfortable doing.

There's no substitute for your own experience. Try thinking in terms of time, not mileage, on your first couple of hikes: Plan to hike a certain number of hours a day, rather than trying to cover a specified number of miles.

Slow down. The ideal pace is one you can sustain for a full day of walking. Don't start out too fast and, when climbing, think in terms of endurance.

Learn the rest step. Useful on steep climbs, the rest step has a jerky stop-and-start gracelessness to it. It looks a little ungainly, but what it lacks in grace, it makes up for in effectiveness.

Eat and drink. Climbs take up a lot of energy, so replenish calories and liquids often. Make sure you drink before a big climb—and carry enough water so you can swill as much as you like when you get to the top.

Take breaks. If you're exhausted, a rest and a snack can do wonders to boost morale. In general, the military adheres to a schedule of 50 minutes of marching to 10 minutes of resting. This is a good pace to start with, although you might find you need more or less rest. During your rest stops, stretch.

Take breaks to enjoy your environment and give your muscles a rest. (Photo: ©Karen Berger/Daniel R. Smith)

GAITERS

When to use. Wear gaiters in tick and rattlesnake country. Elsewhere, they help keep out water, pebbles, cactus quills, grass seeds, dirt, mud, and snow. They are vital in winter, for both warmth and dryness. Good trail, gentle terrain, and good weather render gaiters superfluous. In hot weather, they can make your feet sweaty (and hence contribute to blisters).

Durability and convenience. Gaiters that affix using Velcro are the most convenient for taking on and off. The snap closures used on some models tend to get banged up, and then they either refuse to snap or unsnap. Don't worry about wearing through the strap that fits under your boot: Most gaiters stay at least approximately in place without it. Get in the habit of putting the correct gaiter on the correct foot; that is, so that any buckles are to the outside of your foot. It doesn't make much difference in summer hiking, but if you ever use crampons, you don't want to accidentally step on dangling buckles and straps.

DANCES WITH ROCKS

Ascending scree. Scree is that crumbly, sliding rock rubble you find above tree line. On a steep climb, it's the stuff that slides underfoot and makes you feel that you're going up the down escalator. It's more effective to ascend by switchbacking than to aim straight up. On very steep slopes, kicking steps is somewhat effective. Dig in with your toes, then test to make sure the foothold will hold your weight. One step at a time will get you there.

Descending scree. Once you get the hang of walking on rocks that slide underfoot, experiment with screeing on descents. Screeing works best on steep slopes with deep deposits of crumbly, small rock. It's a little like skiing on your boots. You need to feel as though your center of gravity is right down in your knees. Start skidding down on your heels, and shuffle your feet back and forth in a sliding-running-hopping motion. The goal is a controlled dance with gravity. You can turn (and also slide) from side to side to control your motion. Keep your knees bent, like when you're downhill skiing.

Hiking across talus. Like scree, talus is rock rubble that hangs out on mountainsides. The difference is that talus is the bigger stuff, the piles of rocks and boulders. As with traveling on scree, balance and footing are the major challenges on talus; in addition, watch for falling rock. Hike diagonally across a talus slope rather than straight up or down, and wait to make sure that no one is directly underneath you.

Rock! If you dislodge a rock, don't wait to see where it's headed; yell "Rock!" so that other hikers at least have some warning. If you hear someone call "Rock," resist the temptation to figure out where exactly the rock is coming from. You don't have time. Duck and protect your head.

Advanced talus travel. You've got two choices when descending talus: Go one step at a time, always staying in control (slow and safe and a little bit nerve-wracking) or let 'er rip (safe once you get the hang of it, but nerve-wracking to learn). It's a little like learning to downhill ski: Remember that scary moment when you gave up on the snowplow and headed downhill? This is similar. You have to give up control to gain control.

Try this after you've become comfortable on rock. It's better to start without a pack. Choose a moderate slope to practice on. The idea

Ascending scree, use the rest step to establish a pace you can stick with. (Photo: ©Karen Berger/Daniel R. Smith)

is to sort of float over the rocks, without remaining on any of them long enough to actually have to balance. Think of riding a bike: you're balanced when you're in motion, not when you're still. Look several steps ahead and try to keep your knees bent and your weight right over the balls of your feet. Be ready to move in either direction if the rock underfoot moves. Hiking sticks help. Once you get the hang of it, you can actually travel quite quickly over talus.

SNOW AND ICE

The typical three-season hiker rarely encounters snow that is extensive enough to completely impede forward progress. However, if you are traveling in very high mountains, have begun hiking in spring before the snow has melted off, or have extended your hiking season into the colder months, you'll need to deal—at least sometimes— with the white stuff. Warning: The following hints are for backpackers who occasionally hit patches of snow, not for climbers who deal with much steeper slopes.

Postholing. This is just a fancy name for slogging through deep snow. It's a terribly inefficient way to travel, not to mention exhausting. In very deep snow, abandon the idea of getting anywhere fast. Try to develop a rhythm of kicking forward and then stepping down. A pair of ski poles helps with balance, which will be upset every time your foot steps down and finds something unexpected—a log or a rock— hidden underneath the snow.

Ice. On some mountain slopes, ice lingers well into summer. Before stepping out on a steep icy slope, consider where you're going to end up if you fall. Forget what you've heard about straight lines; sometimes the best way from here to there is a big, round detour. If you must go across and you don't have crampons, consider waiting until later in the day when the ice softens and you can kick steps into it. Soft ice has its own problems, of course—during snowmelt, it weakens and you can fall through a soft spot up to your thighs. But that's safer than losing your footing on ice and taking an unintended, uncontrolled, and possibly fatal slide downhill.

Kicking steps. If you must cross an icy slope without crampons, kick steps. The most effective motion is to think of your knee as a fulcrum and to kick in with your lower leg. Kick into the slope hard, several times for each step. You can also use an ice ax to chop steps into the slope.

Ice axes. These can help you stop a fall—if you know how to use them. Practice self-arrest before you think you'll have to do it.

Crampons. Instep crampons can help you cross the occasional short ice patch, but they are by no means a substitute for full-fledged crampons. Fit them to your boots before you head out. (This goes double for regular crampons.) Sitting on a snowbank with a 200-yard-long ice slope ahead of you is a lousy time to realize that you need an Allen wrench to get those crampons onto your boots. Hint: In soft sun-melted ice, clumps of snow can grow quite large and stick to the crampons (which feels like a tennis ball under your foot). Knock them off by hitting your ice ax against your boot.

Descending snow: the plunge step. This works just like its name implies. It's a little like postholing, only you're going downhill, so gravity comes into play. This is the direct approach. The weight is on the heel, the leg is held straight. Avoid the temptation to go too fast. It's possible to get your leg stuck in a deep hole; if your momentum is too fast, it can carry you forward and you can break your leg.

Crampons give added traction on ice and snow. (Photo: ©Jeff Scher)

Descending snow: boot skiing. The basic idea is to bend your knees and let yourself sort of half slide, half run, shifting your weight from side to side whenever you start losing your balance. A pair of hiking sticks helps.

Descending snow: glissading. This is a fancy name for sliding down on your butt. Control is the key: Most backpacks (especially those with external frames) counter gravity with friction, so if you've got a pack on, you'll be in the slow lane. Gore-Tex or nylon rain pants turn you into a speeding missile. On anything long and steep, you'll want an ice ax for control and braking. Never wear crampons on a glissade; chances are the crampons will catch on some ice or snow, and the result can be a broken leg.

RIVER CROSSINGS

Scout a route. Just because the trail enters the river here and exits it there doesn't mean that the straight line through the middle is the safest place to cross. Make sure that you feel comfortable with the challenges of the crossing. Sometimes this means walking quite a distance along the shore to find a route that looks and feels right. Some people find a slippery log more intimidating than a fast current.

Wide equals shallow. The current is slower and the water shallower in wide places. Also look for spots where the stream splits in two with an island in the middle.

Keeping gear dry. For a truly wet crossing, when you have to swim across or go through deep water, repack your gear for the crossing. The more waterproof stuff sacks, garbage bags, and resealable bags you have, the drier your gear will stay. An inflated air mattress wrapped around your pack and held in place with elastic cords can help make your pack more buoyant.

Unbuckle your waist belt. You need to be able to get out of your pack quickly. If you fall in, your pack could hold you under.

Cross in the morning. This is essential during snowmelt. In spring and early summer, mountain snowfields that feed snowmelt streams freeze (or at least cool down) overnight. In the early hours of the morning, the flow from melting snowfields slows drastically, lowering the water level and calming the flow. In the afternoon, the flow and water level of a snow-fed stream can be multiples higher and stronger—and much more dangerous.

Use walking sticks. If you don't normally carry a walking stick, look along the banks of a river to see if anyone has left one (or two) behind. Using a walking stick (or two) as a third (or fourth) leg helps you keep your footing and balance.

Never walk through white water. Walking through white water can kill you—even in shallow water—if your feet get caught between rocks and the current knocks you over and holds you down. This is one of the cardinal rules of canoeing and kayaking, and backpackers need to heed it, too.

Using trekking poles can help you keep your balance when crossing fast-running streams. (Photo: ©Karen Berger/Daniel R. Smith)

Using fixed ropes. On some hiking trails, ropes have been fixed across the water to aid in fording. Cross on the downstream side. In a really fast current, hold the rope with both hands. It's best not to clip in to the rope; if you slip, the current's force on the rope can hold you under, particularly with a pack on to upset your balance.

▲ ▲ ▲

Tricks with Sticks

You might not appreciate the difference a hiking stick can make until you try it. And two sticks are even better than one. Sticks designed specifically for hiking are available at your outfitters, but you can also use . . .

- A folding wading staff, sold in fly-fishing stores
- Broomsticks with a neoprene grip wrapped around the top (for a handgrip)
- Conveniently sized tree branches
- Bamboo poles (like those from ski areas)

If you buy hiking sticks, get the kind that telescope. You can fold them up and put them in your luggage if you're traveling by plane, and you can telescope them and carry them on your pack if you're on a trail that requires rock scrambling.

Why do you need them?

- To keep your balance on tough terrain
- To help you across a hairy stream crossing
- To save your knees on steep descents
- To test the underbrush in snake country
- To wave aggressively at mean-tempered dogs
- To prop up a ground cloth as a makeshift sunshade during lunchtime
- To whack snow-laden trees in your path so that they dump their load on the ground before you pass under them
- To use as a camera monopod (check to see if your sticks have a universal camera screw)

Use camp shoes. Sharp rocks are a danger, and so are slippery rocks—and the consequences of a misstep are far more serious out in the boonies. Crossing barefoot is out. Using your camp shoes means you won't have to hike in wet boots. The sports sandals favored by rafting guides are amphibious. If you're using sandals that buckle with Velcro and you've had them a while, be sure the Velcro still holds in water, because it tends to wear out faster than the shoe. Small plastic rings are available to hold soon-to-be-retired Velcro straps in place.

Crossing in boots. Changing shoes twenty times in one day is a real time-eater. You can spend 15 minutes on a ford scouting a route, taking your shoes off, getting your stuff together, crossing the stream, drying your feet, and putting it all back the way it was. If the scouting is difficult, it can take much longer. If you're going to have to do several crossings, you might just want to hike in your sports sandals for a while. On a rainy day, when your boots are going to get wet anyway, give up the fight for dry feet. Wring out your socks when the dousing is finally over.

Snow bridges. In late spring and early summer, snow bridges often provide a route across a mountain stream. Look carefully for changes of color, which indicate changes of density in the snow bridge. Don't trust someone else's boot prints as proof that the bridge is safe; boot prints only tell you that the bridge was strong enough to hold the last hiker— who could have passed a day ago, or a week ago. Probe first with a ski pole to make sure the bridge will hold your weight.

NAVIGATION

Heads up! Hey, you at the back of the line! This means you! Don't follow your hiking partners blindly. If the guy in front is daydreaming, you could all end up in the wrong place. Ask questions. "Is that lake we just passed on the map? I don't remember seeing it" is a legitimate query. If you lose the trail, see the tips in the sidebar Finding a Lost Trail.

Watch the blazes. Different hiking trails are marked in a variety of ways: paint blazes, signs, posts, cairns, and ax blazes, to name a few. Some trails are marked every couple of hundred yards; others, only at major junctions. Pay attention to the kind of trail you're on. If it's been marked every few hundred feet and you don't see blazes for a half hour, you might have taken a wrong turn.

Sun and shadow. Your shadow is a handy quick reference that tells you what direction you're going in. A quick glance every now and then can alert you to dramatic wrong turns. How shadows fall depends on the time of day, the time of year, and the latitude. When you start a hike, take a couple of compass readings of where your shadow falls at different times of day to get oriented. After a while, you'll get used to thinking "It's afternoon; if I'm walking west like I'm supposed to be, my shadow is in back of me."

▲ ▲ ▲

Essential Items: Map and Compass

Why do you need them? An abundance of guidebooks and well-marked trails have made map and compass skills a bit of an endangered species. It's possible, for instance, to hike every single one of the Appalachian Trail's 2,160 (as of this writing) miles without even knowing how to use a map and compass! But make no mistake: If a late-season snowstorm covers the trail, an unexpected obstacle blocks the trail, or someone in your group breaks a leg, you need some way to get from where you are to where you want to be. Carry a map and compass, and know how to use them. Local hiking clubs usually offer classes in orienteering.

A Global Positioning System (GPS) receiver, which uses satellite information to pinpoint your exact location, helps. But GPS is a tool, not a skill. Remember: Sensitive electronic instruments can break. Batteries run out or freeze. You can fall on the thing and smash it.

If you're tempted to leave your map and compass home on short, well-marked day-hiking trails, consider a recent news story: A Rhode Island man got lost while leading a group of children on a spring day hike. The group spent the entire night outside without camping equipment in temperatures that dropped into the 40s.

Wear a watch. Knowing what time it is helps you interpret shadows, judge distance, and figure out if you've got enough time to get to your intended campsite (or the next water source) before dark.

Other ways to tell time. In open country where you can see the horizon, stretch out your arm in front of you and hold your hand sideways so that your fingers are parallel to the horizon (thumb down). The number of fingers between the sun and the horizon tells you the time until sunset. Each finger is 15 minutes.

▲ ▲ ▲

Finding a Lost Trail

There are dozens of ways to lose a trail. It could be washed out, blocked by deadfall, obliterated by a mudslide, covered by a late-season snow. Even the best-maintained trails sometimes suffer from the elements. If you lose the trail, stop!

- Look backward. Knowing where you came from can reorient (and reassure) you. Usually there is a beaten path around an obstacle. But before you start beating the bushes, take a good look at your surroundings and pick out some features (a distinctive tree, a fallen log) you can easily recognize and come back to.

- Ask yourself, if you had built the trail, where would it go? Look there for it first.

- Keep your pack on if you're hiking solo. If you're with a hiking partner, you can take your pack off, but stay in calling or whistling distance. Being lost without your pack is a lot worse than being lost with your pack. And in bad mountain weather, fog can come in and disorient you in the space of minutes.

- If going forward doesn't yield an answer, try going back to the last place you were sure was on the trail. You might find that you missed a turn, or a piece of deadfall blocked the route.

- Find the blazes. The problem could be something so simple as a branch that blocks your view. Take a couple of steps to one side and look again from a different angle.

- Use the same technique above tree line. Gray granite cairns can seemingly disappear in a field of gray granite talus. Taking a couple of steps to one side or another often results in a slightly different perspective—and a sight of the missing cairn.

Compass tricks. Get a compass with a folding top, which protects the housing from gumming up with fine particles of dirt and sand. The folding top usually contains a mirror, which can be used as a signaling device.

Other uses for a map. Need to hitchhike back to your car or get help in an emergency? Write your destination on the back of your map in magic marker and use it as a sign. Hikers who know they're going to be hitchhiking back to their car or into town to resupply can make their "signs" before hitting the trail; no need to carry that magic marker! Or the back of your map can also be pressed into service as notepaper. Maps you've finished with can become emergency firestarter (if you're *sure* you're done with them).

LEAVE-NO-TRACE WALKING

Limit group size. Large groups have adverse impact on both the land and on other wilderness users. One person hiking alone sees more wildlife than two people. Two people see more than three people. A group of more than three people is unlikely to see anything at all.

Stay on the trail. Most especially, don't cut switchbacks. Obviously, this is more of a temptation going downhill than going uphill, especially on those western pack trails that swing back and forth as evenly as a pendulum. Switchbacks make for easier climbing, and they also help control erosion on steep slopes. That straight route down the fall line can't handle years of foot traffic and soon turns into an eroded mess.

Hike single file. Trails are cut and constructed for one hiker at a time. They'll last longer, erode less, and look nicer if that's how people hike them.

Shore up water bars. These devices are a simple, low-tech solution to the problems caused by the collusion of water and gravity. Water seeks the quickest course downhill, and a trail very often serves the purpose. Water bars divert water off the trail, which prevents erosion, lengthens the life of the trail, and provides a more even footway. If the drainage is blocked, simply clear it out so that water has an unimpeded route downhill and off the trail. If the water bar is looking a little weak, you can shore it up with dirt and stones.

Walk in the mud. Here's your chance to be a child again. Play in the mud, stomp in the puddles. Go right smack through the middle of the trail instead of cowering on the sides, which widens the trail and turns the area into a big, boggy mess. You can clean up your boots at the evening's campsite.

Weed infestations. In many parts of the country, infestations of hardy exotic species are wiping out local flora. Check with local land management agencies to see if you can do anything; in some cases, they'll ask for a report.

Remove blowdowns. You can't get rid of all of them, but if every hiker removed just one, the trail would be improved.

▲ ▲ ▲

Natural Direction Signs

You've lost your compass and your watch, and the sun's not shining? Here are a couple of other ways to infer direction. Warning: Variances in microclimates can change the way vegetation grows; these are tendencies, not laws.

- Tops of pines and hemlocks point east.
- Barrel cactus leans toward the south.
- Vegetation is more open on north-facing slopes.
- Windblown vegetation bends toward the east (because most weather systems move in from the west).
- Snow is deeper and lingers longer on the north-facing sides of mountains.

Block off shortcuts and social trails. People take shortcuts because they are easy and convenient. If you make them less so by blocking them with a big pile of brush, people are more likely to stay on the real trail.

Make blazes visible. If you have trouble seeing a blaze because shrubbery has grown up in front of it, when you do finally find it, cut or tear away the obscuring vegetation. The next hiker will thank you.

Make the trail visible. Sometimes the trail just isn't clear. There may be social trails, a variety of paths around a blowdown, or an unclear junction. Put some kind of barrier across the wrong way (two or three sticks in a row is the trail community's commonly understood symbol for "don't go here"), and put a small cairn on the right trail.

Hikers wandering off the trail can widen it, causing damage to trailside vegetation. (Photo: ©Dorcas Miller)

Don't build personal trails and cairns. Some hikers leave cairns for their partners. But these impromptu trail markers can confuse people who come after you, especially if they head away from the established, official trail.

Deconstruct rock rings. You can get into a lot of arguments over this. Many hikers feel that a good campsite with a fire ring is a nice thing to find at the end of the day. Fire rings concentrate impact and, in forests below tree line, there are places where fire making is acceptable. But a lake pockmarked with hundreds of rings is a different story. Your sense of aesthetics will tell you when it's time to practice for the next Olympic shot-put competition by hurling fire-ring rocks into the woods.

▲ ▲ ▲

Private Property

Trails need the support of local people, and one of the quickest ways to drive a wedge between local property owners and trail users is to show a lack of respect for their property rights. Unless you have permission from landowners, private property is off limits. This is especially important in cases where new trails are being built, because trail managers might still be in the process of seeking permission or easements from property owners. Landowners are often initially suspicious of trails, thinking that they'll bring in garbage, litter, and liability suits. Your campfire on someone's grazing land during a dry season might well be the reason that a landowner says "no way" to a trail.

Where permission has been granted, hikers should be scrupulous about following the rules. Remember, trails that pass through private property do so because of the goodwill of the landowners. In some cases, property owners have donated easements to a trail club. When traveling across private property, stay on the trail, close fences, and obey posted requests regarding cooking, fires, stoves, camping—or anything else.

CHAPTER 4

THE COMFORT ZONE

Making Your Home
in the Woods

YOUR CAMPSITE IS your castle. Just think of it as a temporary, portable kind of castle. And campsites, like castles, need to be comfortable, secure, and—why not?—even a touch luxurious. Whether you sleep in a lean-to (those three-sided shelters found on many major established trails), a tarp, an improvised shelter, a snow cave, a quinzee, a traditional tent, or simply on a ground cloth thrown down beneath the stars, you want your home for the night to offer the protection the elements require, and a few creature comforts besides: say, a comfortable rock to sit on, a convenient place to cook, clean water, privacy, and, while we're at it, a view of the sunset.

FINDING THE PERFECT CAMPSITE

Use your map. A topo map can tell you not only where to walk, it can help you find a place to camp. Look first for widely spaced contour lines; failing that, look for wildly irregular contour lines. Where the land stops going down and starts going up, there's generally a flat spot in between. Places where you might find these include two water sources coming together, changes from upslopes to downslopes, and flat areas around lakesides. You'll also find flat spots at the top of most passes, but avoid these: They tend to have a wind-tunnel effect and no nearby water. The least likely area to find a flat spot is (no surprise here) when the trail slabs across the side of a hill where, even if the contour lines on the map do flatten out, the land is likely to be consistently canted. In the field, you'll almost always find many more opportunities than the map can show. The most important question to ask your map: If you pass up this great-looking campsite right here, where is the next place to get water, and are you likely to find a flat spot nearby?

Check the guidebook. Most guidebooks describe officially designated campsites. Some also describe unofficial but commonly used sites. Your reaction to guidebook-approved campsites might be to take advantage of their amenities (fire rings, good flat spots, bear boxes or bear poles for hanging food)—or to hike as fast as you can in the opposite direction. Expect to have to share designated or described camping areas with other parties of backpackers, and expect the local wildlife to visit. As far as they are concerned, a couple of flashlights or candle lanterns in an oft-used site is a blinking neon sign announcing "Fast Food Central."

Scout with your pack off. At the end of a hiking day with 40 pounds on your back, any place that is even halfway flat is going to look good. So take your pack off one last time and go scouting so you don't miss out on the really good site just 100 yards away.

Choosing a campsite. If your sleeping pad is your mattress, think of the ground under your tent as your bed frame. The most comfortable is made of sand, gravel, forest duff, mineral soil, or pine needles. The worst is a meadow. Sure, meadows look comfy and soft, but actually, they're likely to be buggy, boggy, and bumpy. You'll be sleeping on a *de facto* sponge, so if it rains, you may find yourself in a puddle. In addition, they are more fragile (hence, apt to be damaged by the wear and tear of hikers tromping around in a campsite). Another vulnerable area to avoid is the grassy tundra above tree line, where tiny alpine flowers and scrub vegetation eke out precarious livelihoods. Choose instead tougher gravel: Under a mattress you'll find that it's more comfortable to sleep on a flat bed of stones than it is to sleep on hummocky grass.

Low-impact tip: campsites and water. Wherever you camp, make sure that your campsite is at least 200 feet from water. This ensures that the debris of your camping activities (even the most rigorous low-impact campers leave some waste behind) doesn't make it into a water source, and it avoids scaring wildlife away from their water. Similarly, make sure you haven't selected a spot that is right in the middle of a game trail. Some animals may be too shy to approach a campsite, and that could mean they'll go thirsty if you are camped between them and the water they depend on. Special care is required in fragile areas like deserts and alpine tundra, particularly around springs.

Low-impact tip: established sites. Here's an easy, logical rule of thumb: In heavily used areas, use established sites. In pristine areas, use dispersed camping techniques and camp out of sight from the trail. Here's why: In popular camping areas, established sites concentrate

Low-impact tip: Use established sites whenever possible to concentrate damage in one area. (Photo: Jeff Scher © ERG)

impact. It's more aesthetically pleasing to come to a lake with ten or twelve heavily used sites than it is to come to a similar lake with signs of a hundred different sites scattered every which way, sometimes only a few yards from each other. In pristine areas, make your camp and when you're done clean up after yourself so no one will know you were there. Give the land a chance to recover from any damage, and the next time a party comes through, they should see no evidence of your site. Without a cleared tent site or fire ring to lure them in, they'll pass right by and make camp somewhere else.

Choosing your bed. Unless you are on a trail that is cutting across a slope, you can almost always find a nearby flat place to camp. On rare occasions, the ground is too rocky or hummocky or densely vegetated and you'll have to walk a while before you can call it quits for the day. Shadows can make a flat spot look crooked—and vice versa, so once you've found a possible site, check the slope by putting down your ground cloth and lying on it. Also, feel for any rocks and bumps that might poke you awake at night. (Don't worry about little bumps; your air mattress will handle a few roots and almost-but-not-quite-buried rocks just fine.)

Sticks and stones can break your bones. Look up! Scree-shouldered mountain slopes frequently pay a tax to gravity and send rock missiles hurtling downward. Dangerous rocky areas advertise themselves with debris. Look for shelter (behind, for instance, a house-sized rocky outcropping) or choose a different campsite. Below tree line, keep an eye out for widow-makers (dead trees that have started to fall but are held up by the branches of other trees). In high winds, be especially careful in forests that have suffered fire damage or insect infestation.

Drainage and slope. Pick a site that won't collect water in a downpour. Digging drainage ditches creates an eyesore and leaves lasting impact. In a pinch, you can build a temporary water bar out of rocks and branches—but remember to dismantle it in the morning. In dry country, avoid flash-flood zones, like the sandy creekbed of a canyon.

Storms and wind. In exposed climates, particularly above tree line, look for protection from the prevailing winds. Note obvious signs of storm and wind patterns: the wind-sheared shape of the Krummholz

Wind-flagged trees indicate the direction of strong prevailing winds. (Photo: ©Dorcas Miller)

(the crooked dwarf evergreens you see on exposed mountains), the contours of snowdrifts, and the patterns of wind-flattened grasses are obvious and reliable indicators. Try to find shelter—behind a rock or inside a grove of trees.

Low-impact tip: camp shoes. Once you choose a campsite, change into camp shoes right away. It's easier on your feet and on the earth. *Don't* go barefoot.

▲ ▲ ▲

Camp Shoes

Camp shoes are low impact: That's low impact on the land and low impact on your feet—a great combination. After a day in hiking boots, you'll appreciate having something lighter to slip into.
- Amphibious sports sandals are the number-one backcountry choice. They're light, airy, and comfortable.

And multipurpose: If your boots blow out (or blister), you can hike in them, at least for a while. They're great for stream crossings. And on long hikes, you can wear them in town.

- Try aqua-socks—the kind divers use. They weigh next to nothing. Two disadvantages: You can't walk far in them, especially on rocky ground. And they look frankly stupid in towns.
- An old pair of sneakers (preferably lightweight) protects the toes of those who don't look where they're going. The disadvantage: If they get wet, they take time to dry.
- Down or synthetically insulated booties are essential in the wintertime. They keep your toes warm and let you walk around camp. Get the ones with some sort of tread on the bottom.

TENT TIPS

Squeezing into a small area. Small tents are more versatile than big tents; free-standing tents are easier to put up than tents that need to be staked. Think small. Your flat spot needs to be only the size of the people who will be sleeping on it. If you're hiking solo, you need a flat spot the size of your body—not the whole tent. Your backpack won't mind snoozing on a few bumps or a downhill slope. A lightweight two-person tent can squeeze into remarkably tiny places. If in doubt, lie down and check. On sloping ground, look for groves of trees, and scout uphill from the big ones, whose roots and trunks sometimes catch eroding dirt, forming a flat place big enough for a tent. Make sure tree branches don't scrape against the tent; if they do, move the tent or gently tie back (do not break off) the branches with a piece of cord.

How to ventilate and be prepared for rain, too. With some tents (like the popular three-pole wedge design), simply attach the rain fly at the foot of the tent. Stretch the fly out as if you were going to put it over the whole tent. Once you've got it in place, roll it back neatly. Tuck the rolled-up fabric in at the bottom of the tent near the poles.

If a storm comes in, you'll be able to unroll the fly into place in a matter of seconds.

A tent with a view. If it's a calm, warm night, pitch your tent with an eye toward views, sunsets, or sunrises—whichever you prefer. Facing the sunrise helps warm your tent in the morning.

Escaping the bugs. Bugs are worst on a warm, humid, muggy night when the air is still. These are the nights to look for a breeze, so head for an exposed knoll or the tunnel effect of a saddle between two hills, and pitch your tent face to the wind.

Know local weather patterns. Generally in the United States, weather comes in from the west, but this is a pretty broad generalization. Find out what the local weather patterns are (thunderstorms in the afternoon, fog by late morning, rainy season in August).

Tenting against the wind. Set your tent so that the wind is at the back (i.e., the low end). If possible, back the tent into a clump of bushes, or hide it behind a rock redoubt. On very windy days with a storm threatening, your priorities are—in this order—finding shelter from

Even in an exposed area, you can often find some protection from the wind. Here, the tent on the left is sheltered by the shrubs. (Photo: ©Karen Berger/Daniel R. Smith)

the wind, pitching your tent with its back to the wind, finding the perfect flat spot. In an all-out mountain gale, sacrifice flatness for protection: You'll get a much better—and safer—night's sleep.

▲ ▲ ▲

At Stake: A Good Night's Sleep

There are two reasons to stake down your tent: to keep it from blowing away, and to make sure the rain runs off of it. Rain flys are designed to shed water when they are staked out; if they just hang down, alternately flapping in the wind and sticking to the tent body, they leak. But staking can be easier said than done, especially when the hard ground of Old Rocky Top threatens to turn a tent stake into a twisted swizzle stick. That's if you're lucky enough to drive it in in the first place.

- If your tent site is large enough to give you a little leeway, test out the ground for "stakability" before you put up the tent—especially if the tent is not freestanding. If you can't gently twist the tent stakes into the ground, forget being subtle and use a fist-sized rock to pound them in.
- Pack mismatched tent stakes—several wimpy ones, one or two sturdier corkscrew stakes, a couple of plastic stakes, and a spare. That way, if one of your stakes just won't go in, you can try a different one. The much-maligned wimpy stakes provided by tent manufacturers actually work well in some rocky ground, where finesse sometimes works better than force. It can be almost impossible to force in a fatter, heftier stake.
- If the ground thwarts your staking attempts, try using above-the-ground alternatives like rocks and tree branches. Extra lengths of parachute cord help extend your guy line so you can tie it off to something solid, even if it's a few yards away.
- Little plastic sliding gizmos (available at your outfitters) can tighten or loosen your guy lines. So can adjustable knots. If you're no good at knots, simply knot your guy lines so they

are divided into sections of various sizes. This gives you several convenient places to try staking.

- If you can't drive in a stake and there's nothing to tie off to, improvise by filling a stuff sack with sand or stones. Clip or tie the end of the guy line to the draw cord of the stuff sack; then set the stuff sack on the ground.
- Snow stakes are wider and flatter than regular stakes. If you don't have them, use ski poles, skis, or ice axes. Or fill a stuff sack with snow and bury it.
- On a wooden tent platform, you may find missing, broken, badly located, or nonexistent guy-line hooks. Find a stick and jam it at an angle between the floorboards, then tie off your guy line to the stick.

Guy lines. The fact that it isn't windy when you set up camp is not a guarantee that it won't become windy in the middle of the night. Setting up your tent as securely as possible means you won't have to crawl out of your tent half asleep when the weather changes in the middle of the night.

Ground cloths. Use a space blanket, an old poncho, or a so-called "footprint" (it's designed by the tent maker to exactly fit the tent's dimensions). Ground cloths go underneath the tent, not in the tent, to protect the more expensive tent floor from being cut up by rocks and roots. If your ground cloth is bigger than your tent, fold up the extra and tuck it underneath. If you don't, the ground cloth will collect and funnel water when it rains, and you'll wake up doing the breaststroke.

Lighten up! Some tents are designed so that you can pitch the rain fly on the poles without using the tent body. This lightweight option provides excellent rain protection and ventilation—but no bug protection.

TARPS

Practice first. There are dozens of ways to rig a tarp, a ground cloth, or a rain poncho to provide protection against sun, wind, or rain. But

Tarps can provide good shelter. There are lots of ways to rig them, but it's best to practice at home first. (Photo: Dave Getchell © ERG)

this is one of those "experience is the best teacher" things. The most important tarp trick is to have done it before you need to. Once you've learned the basics, you can start creatively experimenting with different shapes and techniques, using rocks, tree branches, hiking sticks, and various lengths of rope to devise different configurations.

Sunshades. A standard ground cloth can be pitched as a sunshade if you're hiking somewhere where the midday sun is fierce.

Quick fixes. To jury-rig a grommet, simply put a pebble, acorn, or coin where you need one; wrap a little of the tarp, ground cloth, or plastic sheeting around the hard object, and tie around it with a string.

Hammocks. A hammock-and-tarp combination is a terrific lightweight alternative for below–tree line camping. You don't even need a flat spot; you can set up camp literally anywhere there are two trees.

USING LEAN-TOS

The best room in the house. If you're first into a lean-to, take advantage of your early arrival by choosing a sleeping spot near a wall. Check out the floor for water stains that indicate you're putting your down sleeping bag directly under a hole in the roof.

Weatherproofing. Lean-tos typically have a floor, a roof, and three walls, with the fourth side open. That makes them well ventilated, and it gives you more of the sense of being outdoors than does a tent. But when a wind-driven rain starts falling sideways or you find a quarter inch of snowy spindrift accumulated on your not-really-waterproof sleeping bag, you might want to give yourself some added protection. Hang your ground cloth over the open side—or at least part of it. Tie it on all sides as securely as possible, or it will flap around all night, making noise without doing much to break the wind. Or put up your

Hikers generally covet the space next to a wall in shelters. If you get there first, be economical with space, for other hikers will certainly appear. (Photo: ©Jeff Scher)

tent, which will break the wind and add warmth. Note: Good manners dictate this to be an emergency strategy. A tent pitched inside a shelter makes later arrivals feel distinctly unwelcome. Make room for them immediately, even if that means taking down your tent.

Organize your stuff. Your water bottles, socks, sandals, and flashlights probably look just like everyone else's. When you arrive, assume you'll have company in the shelter and try to keep your things in one central location. When the summer-camp group arrives, you'll at least be able to hang onto what's yours.

Shelter etiquette. On most trails, lean-tos are intended to be temporary shelter for hikers on the move. Your stay should be limited to one night, unless you're hiking off season or in bad weather. Usually, shelters have a designated number of spaces, which may be noted in guidebooks, and space is first-come, first-served. But regardless of the number of people the shelter is designed to hold, trail etiquette follows the Golden Rule: In bad weather, there is *always* room for one more.

Quiet hours. Hikers are distinctly diurnal animals. An hour after dark, the only sounds emanating from most shelters are an assortment of snores interrupted by zippers being undone to accommodate late-night calls of nature. Similarly, most hikers are up by dawn; some rise an hour before sunrise in order to be walking with first light. If your schedule is different (you intend to turn your stove on at 4:00 A.M. to get an early start on a record 40-mile day, or you expect to sleep undisturbed till noon), don't stay in the shelters.

LITTLE CRITTERS

In shelters. Trail shelters usually have a couple of permanent residents. Among the ones I've been personally introduced to (sometimes at very close quarters at very wee hours) are porcupines, birds, bats, mice, chipmunks, weasels, skunks, raccoons, and (once, under the floorboards) a rattlesnake. They're there to steal your food. Most lean-tos have dozens of heavy-duty nails pounded into the rafters and roof beams. Hang up your food bags, along with anything that might be mistaken for food (toothpaste, lotions, your as-clean-as-you-can-get-them cooking utensils, garbage) on the nails that stick out from the rafters of most shelters.

Use food storage bins. If your campsite or shelter has some sort of official or improvised contraption for hanging or otherwise protecting food, you can assume there's a pretty good reason. Use it! The more frequently used your campsite is (and, by definition, this is especially true for shelters), the more frequently you will hear the scuffling and scraping of small animals trying to get their teeth into your food. Generally, this happens at 3:00 A.M.

Natural-fiber alert! Mice like cotton T-shirts and bandannas. Also wool socks. No, they don't parade around in mouse-sized outdoor fashions. They rip and shred wool and cotton clothing for use in their nests, especially in winter. Don't leave natural-fiber clothing lying out at night.

▲ ▲ ▲

Anti-mouse Contraption

It's nothing short of amazing how creative animals can be when they have all day to figure out how to get at your food. Shelter mice are veritable geniuses. Foil them with a stick, a string, and an empty can. Here's how:

- Tie a piece of cord (2 to 3 feet is plenty) from a beam or protruding nail.

- Punch a hole into the center of the bottom of an empty can of any size. Hold the can upside down, run the cord through the hole, then knot it under the can so that the can is resting against the knot, about 1 foot lower than the beam or branch.
- Tie the remaining cord around the middle of a sturdy stick a few inches lower than the can. A stick ½ inch in diameter and 8 to 12 inches long is a good size, but you can make do with whatever you have.
- Hang your stuff sacks from the stick. The mice can climb down the string—but they can't get over the can.

Save your pack! Wherever you leave your pack for the night, open all its pockets (even if you're laying the pack on the ground outside your tent and it's covered with your pack cover). Animals will be able to explore to their heart's content without feeling the need to use drastic break-in techniques (teeth and claws).

Porcupines. In porcupine country, hang your boots and pack because porkies love salt, which they find on the sweaty waist belt and shoulder straps of your pack and inside your boots.

BEAR COUNTRY

In the contiguous United States, there are two kinds of bear. Grizzly bears are found primarily in the northern Rockies: The largest populations are in areas in and surrounding Yellowstone National Park and Glacier National Park (along with the adjoining Bob Marshall and Scapegoat Wildernesses).

Black bears are found virtually everywhere, from the New York City suburbs to the mountain passes of the High Sierra. Of the two species, black bear are far more common, and in some densely populated ursine communities, it may not be possible to hike a trail without having to take a firm stand on just who owns that bag full of freeze-dried glop.

Beware the national parks. Partly because there is no hunting in national parks and partly because there is an unending supply of people bringing in food, black bears who are fortunate enough to live in our nation's most dramatic places have developed sort of an attitude about hikers and their food. Take special care in areas controlled by gangster mobs of thieving bruins, especially (but not limited to) Sequoia, Kings Canyon, Yosemite, Shenandoah, and Great Smoky Mountains National Parks. In these heavily used areas, the cumulative effect of too many hikers improperly storing too much food has led to a situation in which bears view hikers as food service providers.

Avoid overused campsites. You can tell if a campsite is overused, right? Well, so can a bear. And a bear knows that, night after night, there are likely to be all kinds of goodies worth making an effort to get to. Avoid the campsites with forty-two fire rings and soil so densely packed it feels like blacktop. The exception: sites with "bear boxes"—usually old ammo cans or metal lockers chained to a tree. The bears may visit, but your food will be safe.

Bear bag first. Sometimes bear bagging takes longer than you think it's going to. Sometimes the "perfect" bear-bagging tree you saw turns out to be not so perfect; the branches are actually too low (or too high or too brushy) or they can't hold up a food bag. In places where bears are so acclimated to humans that they are dangerous pests, set up your bear-bagging rope before you do anything else. Hang up your food, then make camp. When it's time to cook, just let your food down, take out the night's entree, and put the rest of the food back up in the tree where it's safe while you're cooking and relaxing and lolling about your camp.

Bear bagging. When choosing a bear-bagging tree, try to find one without a lot of dense foliage. (Good luck. The perfect bear-bagging tree exists only in the National Park Service's brochures.) You need about 40 feet of rope to bear bag. Carry the heaviest rope you can stand

to put in your pack. You'll understand why when you visit a bear-infested national park and see a spider's web of lightweight rope and parachute cord tangled in the treetops. The heavier your rope, the less likely it is to get tangled. If you're using lightweight rope or cord, compensate by choosing a heavier rock—1 to 2 pounds—as a counterweight. Its momentum may keep the rope from getting stuck in the tree. Figure 2 illustrates how to bear bag with two roughly equal-weight food bags.

What to put in a tree? Anything a bear might want to eat, including toothpaste, garbage, and that candy bar you left in your pack's side pouch.

Bear bagging involves hanging your food out of reach of hungry bruins. (Photo: ©Karen Berger/Daniel R. Smith)

Figure 2. The counterbalance method of bear bagging is the most effective way to foil an uninvited dinner guest.

Carry a carabiner. Keep it tied to the other end of your bear-bagging rope. You can just clip your stuff sacks to the 'biners, rather than fussing with knots.

Above tree line. Line your food sacks with garbage bags and hang them from a rock overhang. Or bury the food sacks under a large cairn (not a great solution: It takes a lot of effort and will not protect your food from small critters like pikas).

Bridges. If you're camped near a bridge, hang your food off the side. Just make sure it's high enough over the water so the bear can't reach it from below.

Use your judgment. Most bear-foiling schemes available at official campsites (bear poles, bear boxes, and the like) are designed to serve the purpose, and do so. But don't let an official amenity substitute for judgment. Make sure the pole provided allows you to hang your food at least 8 feet high (and preferably 10 feet high) and 100 feet from where you are sleeping. If not, go find a tree.

Defending your camp. Pitch your tent so that you can look out and see just exactly what is making that noise underneath your food stash. Keep a pile of stones handy; your pots and pans can be placed under your bear-bagging tree as a sort of burglar alarm. Park rangers who deal routinely with black bears encourage park visitors to take a firm stand with their food, and that includes throwing rocks at an in-vader intent on a midnight snack. Never, under any circumstances, throw rocks at or otherwise confront a grizzly.

Grizzly country. Black bear precautions go double in grizzly coun-try. Never sleep with your food in your tent. Cook and hang food well away from your sleeping area (100 feet or more; see Figure 3). Some hikers also hang the clothing they cooked and ate in.

CAMPING COMFORT

Camp chairs. True, it's a luxury item. But some of them are no more than a couple of ounces (they use your sleeping pad). If you're inclined to sit around in camp a lot, a camp chair can add a nice measure of comfort. Check out the envious glances other hikers cast your way.

Other things to sit on. A butt-sized piece of old foam pad or a plastic placemat takes the annoyances out of small, sharp protrusions. You can use the placemat for food preparation; either can then be used as a shock-absorber for your stove when you're traveling during the day.

Figure 3. A low-impact campsite in bear country. Both your cooking and sleeping areas should be at least 200 feet away from any water and separated from each other.

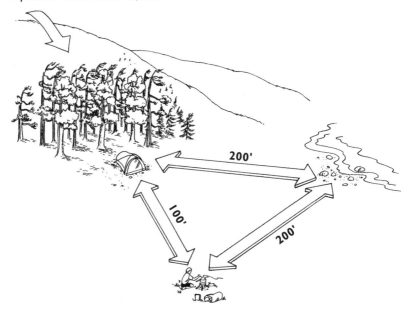

Air mattresses. These are comfortable, but it only takes one almost invisible little hole to defeat their whole purpose. If you sit out on them, be careful where you place them, or put your ground cloth underneath them first.

▲ ▲ ▲

Bear-Bagging Tricks

Getting your rope over a high tree branch takes more than a good arm. The heavier the rope, the less likely it is to get snagged in the tree. Tie the end of the rope to a rock. (This usually means knotting it and wrapping it around the rock a couple of times.) The rock should be about the size of a large grapefruit. But even if you've mastered all your Boy Scout knots, chances are that unless you get the rope over the branch on the first or second try, the knot will work loose and you'll have to tie it again.

If the tree branch is the right height (about 10 to 12 feet) and you've got a straight shot at it (i.e., there aren't a lot of branches in the way), go ahead and use the rock. Make sure the rope ends up at least 4 feet away from the trunk of the tree. But if the only branch in sight is 20 feet high and surrounded by smaller branches, try these tricks to spare you vast amounts of cussing at the trees:

- Instead of tying the rope around a rock, put several smaller rocks into an old sock. Tie the sock to the rope and throw the sock over the tree branch.
- The same idea can also be used with a stuff sack instead of a sock. Put the rocks in a small stuff sack, tie the stuff sack to the rope, and throw the stuff sack over the branch.
- Once the rope is over the tree branch, it may not come all the way down by itself. You can coax it down by working the rope. Jiggle the rope by holding onto it and making a tossing motion in the direction of the tree branch. The rocks' weight will pull the other side down. Repeat until the other end of the rope is within reach.

Organize, organize! Your gear doesn't do you any good if you can't find it. Get in the habit of putting the same things in the same places every day, and use those mesh organizing pockets sewn inside your tent.

SLEEPING COMFORT

Air mattresses. If it's self-inflatable, let it inflate itself. It takes a little time (particularly the full-length ones), but it avoids getting water vapor from your breath inside the mattress. If you blow up your mattress in cold weather, don't be surprised when you enter your tent a couple of hours later to find that it no longer feels fully inflated. No, it hasn't sprung a leak; the volume of your hot breath has decreased as the air has cooled. Just add a couple of puffs and you'll be all set.

Pillows. Blow air into an empty water bag. Use a stuff sack full of clothes. A clean T-shirt can serve as a pillow case. Some sleeping bag stuff sacks now come lined with cushy, comfy fleece.

Extra clothing. Don't be tempted to stuff extra clothing under your sleeping pad if you're camped in a less than perfectly flat spot. On a rainy night, many hikers find that their tents leak a little, and any water that creeps in will end up soaking your spare clothing.

LIGHT

Candles. Fat plumber's candles last longer than the equivalent weight in batteries, you always know how much you have left, and they make good firestarter.

Candleholders. In shelters, flat cans (tuna fish, smoked oysters) make serviceable candleholders. If it's windy, protect the flame with the windscreen from your stove.

Flashlights. This is the only thing to use if you need to walk out at night. At night in your tent, flashlights are much safer than candles. You can create a stable source of light that doesn't bounce around every time you change positions by putting your flashlight in a clear or translucent plastic water bottle.

Headlamps. This is even better than a flashlight. You'll have two hands free for in-camp chores and can direct the light beam where you need it.

Dead battery blues. Flashlights have the annoying habit of switching on when they bump up against something else in your pack. The kind that turn on with a twist of the bulb housing are less prone to sudden fits of lighting up. Three ways to keep flashlights from impulsively declaring "let there be light": tape the switch into the off position, take out the batteries, or put the batteries in a dysfunctional upside-down position.

Before bedtime. Know where you put the flashlight before you go to sleep.

▲ ▲ ▲

Essential Item: Flashlight

Why do you need it? A scenario: You've done everything right. You started early, your pack has the Ten Essentials, and now it's midafternoon and you are bushwhacking up a trailless mountain. Your goal is to get over a pass and down the other side to a clearing where you can camp.

The climb is not particularly tough, but it seems to be eating up the hours. You keep having to detour around impermeable thickets of vegetation. The route is rocky and uneven and you patiently press on, noticing that the shadows are growing longer and longer. You also notice that there is not a single flat spot, or even a sort of flat spot, where you could pitch a tent.

Dusk can come quickly, especially if you run into trouble as the day is drawing to a close. You may need to walk longer than you thought before finding a campsite. You may have to pitch your tent in the dark. You may have to rescue someone.

Pack one flashlight per person, plus extra batteries and bulbs.

SPIRIT LIFTERS AND BOREDOM REDUCERS

Tear and share. If you're a backcountry bookworm, stick with inexpensive paperbacks. Rip off the covers and tear the book into sections. Only take as much of the book as you think you'll be able to read. Pass the sections you've finished reading to your hiking partner. Better yet, read aloud; it takes half the headlamp battery-power and twice the time—which means your book lasts longer. Plus it's a nice way to share. Try choosing a local book about the region you're hiking in.

Read the back of the guidebook. You know, the part with the natural history and the geology. The part that tells you about the land you're walking through.

Bird-watching. Take along a small bird book and learn to identify birds by sight and by call. You don't have to memorize the names of 200 species of birds. Start out by learning a few common species in the area, then add on as you see newcomers. Check out which birds are migrating when.

Stargazing. Nighttime skies in many backpacking areas are much darker than city skies. You'll see details of constellations and the Milky Way and, especially in August, shooting stars. A star chart can help you recognize constellations you don't know. Start with the Big Dipper and the North Star, the most useful star for a backpacker to know.

Plant identification. The mountain laurel of the east, the snow-melt bloom in the summertime Rockies, the rhododendron bloom in the southern Appalachians, the brilliance of autumn foliage—you'll eventually want to know what you're looking at. A plant identification book can tell you just what all those beautiful flowers, leaves, and trees are. If you've got a macro lens on your camera, use it to look up close at a newly unfurling leaf or to photograph the tiny details of a mountain flower. Above all, simply look.

Music. Now's your chance to learn the harmonica. Didn't bring one along? Spoons, pots and pans, or a water bottle full of pebbles can form a rhythm section. Now, if only someone in your group could sing. . . .

Hackey sack. This is for the energetic crowd. The point is to keep the sack in the air. Some backpackers display a curious lack of interest in a game that has them jumping around after a long day of hiking.

Juggling. The basic trick to juggling is easy to learn: Each ball gets thrown up in the air to the other hand, then thrown back up in the air to the first hand. (It's an illusion that the balls go around in a circle.) You can practice with pine cones. Rocks are not recommended.

Miniature travel games. These reduced-in-size magnetic travel games are compact and lightweight and worth their weight in entertainment. They usually contain several different games.

Board games. Photocopy the boards at a reduced size, then laminate them. You can make checkers or backgammon pieces out of pebbles or scraps of paper. Or draw a board in indelible ink on your bandanna.

Paper games. Tic-tac-toe and hangman only require a piece of paper. Improvise word games. Try taking turns picking a word and then seeing who can make the most words out of the letters in it.

Playing cards. A deck of cards can help you happily waste hours of time—even if you're hiking solo. Remember solitaire?

CLEANLINESS AND HYGIENE

Human waste disposal. Disposing of human waste properly is the most important thing you can do to leave no trace. Always carry a trowel and dig a cat hole 6 inches deep, at least 200 feet away from any water source (about 70 paces for an adult). Choose a place that is not visible from the trail or campsite, and isn't likely to be stumbled upon by the next camper.

Personal cleanliness. Okay, so it's a hiker's prerogative to smell like week-old sweat socks. But plunging into a cold mountain lake makes you feel terrific at the end of a day—and it'll keep your sleeping bag cleaner, which means you will have to wash it less frequently, which means it will last longer.

Use a sleeping bag liner. A lightweight silk or nylon liner feels better than the stuff your sleeping bag is made of, and it protects the bag from your dirt and sweat.

Backpacking towels. A sure sign of a neophyte backpacker is a big ole bath towel hanging off the back of a pack to dry. But some experienced hikers just can't, or prefer not to, live without something with which to dry off. Try a bandanna, a terry face cloth, a dish towel, or one of the super-absorbent backpacking towels you can buy at outfitters. They absorb several times their weight in water. A white or light-colored towel dries faster than a dark one; small white hotel-type towels are lightweight and fast-drying.

Sun showers. On a warm day, put your dark-colored waterbag in direct sun and let it soak up the rays. You can't really call it a hot shower—but it'll be warm enough. If you really get into the idea, outfitters sell various tube and valve adaptations to turn your water sack into a real backwoods shower system. And if the sun doesn't heat the water sufficiently, add some boiled water.

When you break camp, give your tent a good shake to get rid of any dirt. (Photo: Jeff Scher © ERG)

Favorite cleaners. Multipurpose soaps aren't fancy, but one little bottle will serve for skin, hair, dishes, and clothes. Make sure it's biodegradable. Liquid soaps are easier to handle in the woods than cakes of soap, which have an inordinate fondness for falling in the dirt.

Low-impact tip: washing. Don't do your washing—of self, dishes, or clothes—directly in a water source. Just because your soap is biodegradable doesn't mean that someone downstream wants to drink it! Bring water to washables (your camp should be at least 200 feet from the water source)—not the other way around. Letting wash water drain through the soil has less impact than dumping it straight in a stream or spring. Also, your waste-water disposal area should be at least 100 feet from your camping area.

Rinse-free bathing. Soaps, shampoos, and conditioners that don't require rinsing out are available.

FOR WOMEN ONLY

Something everyone wonders about and no one discusses: What do you do during "that time of the month?" The answer: Don't sweat the small stuff. Dealing with menstruation in the woods is more an attitude than anything else. There's no reason not to spend any day of the month in the backcountry. The old myth that menstruating women should avoid hiking in grizzly country is just that—a myth. Bear experts at Yellowstone National Park say there is no evidence to support this common misconception. Of course, you'll want to sleep well away from any garbage related to your period.

Don't be caught by surprise. Hiking is a change of environment and it's physically stressful; just like jet lag, it can alter your monthly cycle. So no matter when you're heading out, take along enough supplies and any medications you usually use.

Resealable plastic bags are a woman's best friend. Keep them handy (along with toilet paper and your choice of sanitary supplies). Store the waste in the bags until you reach a garbage bin. It's a good idea to keep resealable bags and toilet paper handy even when you're not menstruating, for the obvious reasons: You don't have to dig in your pack and you can take care of bathroom needs without a lot of fuss. And you stay a lot cleaner if you use toilet paper.

Moist towelettes. A couple of baby wipes or moistened towelettes really make a difference, especially when you're hiking in hot, dry country.

Packing it out. To cut down on odors, some people put a cotton ball soaked in ammonia in the plastic bag they intend to use for garbage. Another, more convenient, strategy: Use a small baggie for your daily supply of garbage, then put it into another, larger bag at the end of the day. The next day, start another small baggie for garbage. At night, hang these bags out of reach of animals and far from your tent. Don't forget to pack them out.

Burning garbage. Even the most minimum impact–conscious of us occasionally makes a fire. Women are well advised to time their pyromaniacal impulses to their menstrual cycle. You can burn personal sanitary supplies, but it takes a fairly serious fire. Make sure the fire has done its job before you leave the campsite, and pack out anything that didn't completely burn.

Never bury sanitary supplies. Animals will dig them up. Yech.

Tampons. If you use tampons with applicators (a little easier, considering the awkward position you have to assume in the absence of a toilet), choose cardboard ones that you can burn, rather than plastic ones.

Wear pads. You may not use them at home, but in the woods, they prevent accidents and eliminate the inconvenient necessity of an emergency trip *right this very second*, whether or not there's a rock or bush to hide behind. On well-traveled trails, they're a lifesaver. And at night, they reduce the possibility of making a mess in your sleeping bag. Use them alone or in conjunction with tampons—whatever your preference is.

Carry several different-colored bandannas. You can use different-colored ones for different jobs. Reserve one for personal cleanup.

CHAPTER 5

AT THE CHUCKWAGON

—

Backcountry Cookcraft

PACKING THE RIGHT food is only half the equation. At the end of the day, you've got to cook it. Simple as most backpacking fare is, like any other food you eat, it benefits from the right equipment and a little technique—which becomes all the more important when you're cooking under a steadily darkening sky.

COOK KITS AND UTENSILS

Improvising. Check your kitchen before you buy new camping equipment. An aluminum pie plate works as a pot lid and a saucepan. The beat-up little pot you never use at home might live out its life in the woods. And those reusable plastic containers that take-out food comes in these days make convenient dishes.

How much stuff? It depends on the size of your group, whether you intend to cook together, and whether you're willing to stagger cooking and eating times. Generally, one backpacking stove holds a pot that can handle dinner for two hikers at a time.

Pot scrubbers. Although it comes in handy for stubborn, stuck-on black gunk, steel wool is too messy to use every day because it starts to rust and fall apart when wet. Instead, try nonrusting alternatives or a scouring pad. Forget about a sponge; it's not up to the job, and it starts stinking after a day in your pack.

Pot grabbers. When cooking, get into the habit of remembering where you set down your pot grabber. But if yours does wander off for a predinner stroll of its own, use a wool sock or a wadded-up bandanna to rescue your over-boiling dinner.

Drinking cups. The classic metal Sierra cups lose heat almost immediately, and when they are hot, they're too hot to hold. They are, however, good for day hikes, because in an emergency, you can cook up a cup of hot water in them. They're also convenient when you need to scoop water out of a shallow stream. For hot drinks and soups in camp, most backpackers prefer an insulated plastic mug.

Bowls. Some kind of plastic bowl is ideal. If you're hiking solo, skip the bowl and eat out of the pot, assuming you're doing one-pot meals. More complicated recipes require more complicated equipment.

Eating utensils. Take a spoon. Nothing you're going to eat in the backcountry requires a fork. If you insist on a fork, you can buy a sort of fork-spoon combination (the spoon's bowl is edged with a couple of tines) in outfitting stores.

▲ ▲ ▲

Essential Item: Pocket Knife

Why do you need it? Pocket knives come in handy for a whole range of tasks, including whittling down wet wood to make dry kindling, cutting strips of cloth into bandages, removing splinters, gutting a fish, cutting cheese and sausage, and opening cans. Swiss Army–type knives tend to be popular and long-lasting, but don't succumb to the temptation of those heavyweight jobs that have a hundred different blades. Hikers differ on the required features of the perfect backcountry knife, but popular ones include scissors, can opener, bottle opener, tweezers, awl, standard blade, screwdriver, and, for the sybarites among us, a corkscrew.

FIRES

Low-impact tip: no fires. Minimum impact says no to most recreational fires. In heavily used areas, campsites are scarred with a series of fire rings—sometimes a hundred or more around a popular lake. In heavily used areas, especially fragile ecosystems like alpine meadows, avoid making fires. Plus, it's just common sense that it's easier to cook on a stove. For one thing, you don't run the risk of your dinner falling into the fire.

Acceptable fires. If you must cook on a fire, build a small one on mineral soil. Another good place: under the water line of a river that's at low flow (or low tide for an ocean campsite). Or choose a campsite with a pre-existing fire ring. If there are multiple scars or rings, use the most logical one, scattering the other rings to avoid the unnecessary charred sites. Make sure fires are permitted in the area where you're camping. Also make sure that forest fire conditions aren't hazardous. (See Figure 4.)

A tripod fire. Collecting fuel wood is a major chore in less-developed countries, so local cooks don't waste a single piece. Here's how they make a small, efficient fire that offers a stable place on which to cook the family meal. Find three rocks of roughly equal size. (Don't take them from a riverbank; stones containing moisture can explode in a fire.) Place the stones in a small triangle and set your pot on them to make sure it sits evenly. Then make a small fire between the three stones using sticks about a finger's-diameter wide. When you have a bed of coals, set the cookpot on the stones. If you need to feed the fire, slip a few small pieces of wood underneath the pot as needed.

Windy days. Don't build a fire on windy days, especially in dry country where forest fire danger is high. If you build a fire in a low breeze, make sure it is downwind of your tent or sleeping area. It only takes one flying ember to irreparably damage an air mattress.

Match storage. Remember what you learned last time you bought a computer: back it up! Take along a couple of new packs of matches (waterproof, windproof, or waxed are best) in double layers of self-locking plastic bags. Store them in different stuff sacks

Figure 4. A low-impact way to make a small cook-fire is to build it in a pie-sized aluminum pan.

in different parts of your pack. Replace the plastic bags when they get holes in them. And take a cigarette lighter—just in case. Overkill? Not when your pack gets accidentally but completely dunked in a river. Or when it's been raining for 3 days.

Wood sense. Lightweight wood burns faster; denser wood burns longer. If wood is damp and you manage to get a fire going, stack the wood you've collected close to the fire so it can dry out before you use it.

▲ ▲ ▲

Essential Items: Firestarter and Matches

Why do you need them? You need firestarter and matches for the same reason you need a flashlight: In case things don't go exactly as you planned.

If you're lost, a signal fire at night can be seen for miles. A fire can keep you warm. (Even the work of building a fire can keep you warm.) A fire enables you to make hot drinks, even if all you have is water and a Sierra cup. (A Sierra cup isn't one of the Ten Essentials, but it's handy to have.)

The way things work, you tend to need fires most just when they're the most difficult to build—like in a 50-degree downpour. Keep your matches in a double layer of resealable plastic bags or a waterproof container. Ditto for firestarter. Throw in a cigarette lighter for good measure.

Here are some tips on firestarters:

- Take along commercially made firestarter: tubes of fire-ribbon, little balls of wax and sawdust, and petroleum-based tablets will all get even a dripping-wet piece of wood to light.
- Make your own with a cardboard egg carton. In each hole, put a little crumpled-up newspaper and melted wax. (Sawdust works, too.) When the wax hardens, you've got a dozen firestarters.
- Use a candle.
- So what to do if you've used all the firestarter because it's been raining for a week? Check your pockets: The instructions that come with your clothes dryer tell you to

remove the lint from the lint screen because it's a fire hazard. Just what you want when you're stuck in the rain in outer-nowhere! If you're the planful type, take some along. If not, check inside the pockets of your wool shirt or fleece jacket.

- Nature provides, too. Try pine needles, birch bark, and standing dead wood. Look for dry wood near the base of trees, under protected rock ledges, and in tree hollows. Whittle down a larger piece of not completely soaked wood to get at its probably dry center.
- Make sure you have enough dry kindling and tinder before you try to start the fire. Once you get a flame, you need to concentrate on building the fire up until it's self-supporting, and to do that, you need dry fuel readily available.

STOVES

Which kind? One way to choose your stove is on the basis of the type of fuel that's available where you plan to travel. You can usually find bottled gas for sale at public campgrounds. If you've got a multifuel stove, you can fill 'er up at the local gas station. Check local guidebooks to see if they have a recommendation. Remember, you can't take fuel on planes.

Read the directions. Seemingly small adjustments can make a world of difference in efficiency and durability. Try the stove out at home (outside) before you take it into the backcountry. Take the directions into the field with you so you have a prayer of fixing whatever goes wrong.

Kerosene. This fuel is widely available worldwide, but it burns dirty and is difficult to ignite. You can hold a match to it until the match burns your fingers, and if you dip the match into the kerosene by accident, out goes the match.

Prime with alcohol. Alcohol is something that should be in your first-aid kit, anyway. You can store it in a teeny little plastic bottle with a squirter cap. Priming with alcohol causes less flare-up. And if you add a couple of drops to kerosene, you can actually get the darn stuff to light.

A flat rock is a great place to make a backcountry kitchen. (Photo: ©Karen Berger/Daniel R. Smith)

Dry-cleaning fluid. Petroleum-based dry-cleaning fluid is actually white gas. In other countries, it's quite readily available, whereas white gas (and even, sometimes, automobile gas) is difficult to find near a trailhead.

Don't overload the stove! Big pots and small stoves often conspire to put your dinner in the dirt. Use a reasonable 2-quart pot. And make sure the stove is stable before lighting up.

Protect the stove. When you put it in your pack, wrap something soft around it—maybe a piece of foam pad—or be sure it's surrounded by softer things that will absorb any shocks and bounces.

Packing fuel. Keep gas upright in your pack. It's extremely unlikely to spill, but you might as well minimize the chance. With

Whisperlite-type stoves, make sure the tube that transports gas from the bottle to the stove isn't leaking a little before you put it away.

Z-zip stoves. The fuel for these stoves is wood. You collect little bits of wood and bark, arrange them in the burner, and turn on a battery-powered fan. If you're using a Z-zip stove, take along a little resealable bag in which you can collect pieces of highly flammable tinder. That way, you'll have a starter stash of dry stuff in case it rains.

Reuse hot water. If you're concerned about fuel consumption (especially in cold weather), choose foods that require less hot water (thin noodles over thick; rice rather than pasta). Or reuse the pasta-cooking water (which is full of vitamins and carbohydrates) in hot chocolate or soup.

The humble one-pot meal. It requires less fuel to cook it, and it stays hotter longer.

Instant soups or quick-cooking Asian noodles. Just boil 'em and eat 'em. The directions on some noodle packages tell you to boil for 3 minutes; it's not necessary. Bring water to a rolling boil. Put the noodles in. Once they return to a boil, take them off the heat. They'll soften up just fine in a couple of minutes.

▲ ▲ ▲

Stove Efficiency

Windscreens. They increase efficiency, which means you have to carry less fuel. Use them, even if there's no wind. Same goes for the heat reflector. Windscreens go around the flame and the pot—*not* the fuel source (see Figure 5).

Heat exchangers. These are round, accordion-folded pieces of metal that slip around your pot (see Figure 5). They channel the heat more efficiently and save their weight in fuel.

Filter the gas. Stoves, like cars, run better on better gas. Run white gas through a mesh filter to strain out any impurities. And if your stove comes with little filters to put on the gas intake tube, use them.

White gas stoves and fuel. Don't completely fill the fuel tank: leave at least 1 inch of air space. Some stove manufacturers

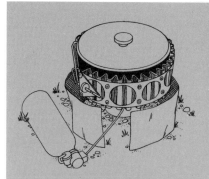

Figure 5. The most efficient way to set up a stove is to use a windscreen and a heat exchanger and to cover the pot with a lid. Some models have a heat reflector around the bottom of the stove.

recommended filling the fuel to no more than three-quarters full.

Blacken the cook pot. Cook over a fire—not always, just the first meal. That baked layer of black soot helps your pot get hotter faster on a stove. A permanent layer of baked-on soot isn't pretty, but it traps more heat than a shiny-clean surface.

Always use a lid. It speeds the process and, more importantly, saves fuel. If you're buying a cook kit, choose one that has a lid that can double as a frying pan or sauce warmer.

White gas stoves. Blow out the yellow flame that lingers after you shut off the stove. It serves no purpose, and it clogs the jet.

Oil the pump cup. The pump cup is the little leather pumping device at the bottom of the shaft of the pump. If it's not oiled, it dries up and you won't have any way to pressurize the stove. Mineral oil is best; any kind of oil, including petroleum jelly or lip balm, is better than none.

FOUL-WEATHER CUISINE

Don't cook in your tent. Flares, melted tents, fires, and asphyxiation are four good reasons to never ever cook in your tent. Backpackers almost never encounter the kinds of conditions that can drive a Himalayan climber into a tent for days on end. Prime the stove outside the tent (that means outside the vestibule, too) and, when it is chugging along like it's supposed to, with no signs of temper tantrums, pull it inside the vestibule. Not the tent.

Easy does it. Choose your simplest meal for rainy-day cooking. On a really foul day, even just-add-water meals taste great.

Prepare your food first. Do all the cutting, slicing, and mixing you need to, and have your gear organized, before turning the stove on. You won't waste fuel, and you'll spend less time outside fussing with that packet of gravy you forgot to mix up.

Sleep with your fuel. It improves cold-weather stove performance. This is crucial for cartridge stoves, which may not work at all in deep-freeze temperatures. Sleep with the stove, too—or, if it's really intolerably crowded in that sleeping bag, put the stove inside the tent somewhere where it won't get rolled on.

Use a stove pad. A square of foam pad wrapped with duct tape can be a cutting board during food preparation and a stable stove base during cooking, and it will slow down the transfer of heat from hot stove to cold ground. You can also use a mouse pad from your computer.

Keep the fuel cartridge warm. They don't work when they're too cold. You can stick it in the sleeping bag with you, cradle it under your jacket, wrap your warm hands around it, or carefully dunk it into a pot of warm (not hot, and *never* boiling) water. You can keep the bottle warm by wrapping a strip of an old foam pad around the cartridge.

Don't touch the fuel bottle. Bare fingers on cold metal is a recipe for frostbite. Bare fingers on cold metal supercooled by liquid fuel (which is far colder than freezing) is a guarantee of it.

Cooking gloves. Keep a pair of glove liners with your cook kit. If they are polypropylene, be careful, because they burn easily.

Warning. You can use your body heat to warm lots of things: stuck-on water bottle lids, fuel bottles, frozen cans of sardines, peanut butter, or tomato paste. But each time you do, your body is giving up heat.

CLEANUP

Pot scrubber alternatives. After a couple of days of backcountry use, a pot scrubber tends to get a little messy. When you can't stand to touch yours anymore, try natural alternatives like sand from a streambed, a handful of small pebbles, or snow.

Beating the grunge. If you've got caked-on residue from an imperfectly cooked meal, add a little water to the pot, heat it for a couple of minutes, and let it sit and soak while you're eating dinner.

Low-impact tip: doing dishes. What's true for washing your body and your clothes is also true for your dishes: Don't wash them directly in streams. Scour them out and dump the water at least 200 feet away from the stream so it can percolate through the soil. In highly sensitive environments, dishwater that contains food fragments should be strained through a piece of cheesecloth and the bits and pieces should be packed out.

CHAPTER 6

WEATHER

How to Laugh at Stormy Skies

SURE, YOU WANT great days. Who doesn't? But try to avoid the trap of thinking you can only enjoy yourself if the weather is good. Part of the backpacking process is learning to appreciate and enjoy different kinds of weather.

Of course, the more comfortable you are, the happier you'll stay. Here's how.

RAIN

Can you really have a successful hike through a waterlogged weekend? Sure—if you have the right attitude, and if you keep your gear dry. On a cold, rainy, gray-skied day, most hikers take great comfort in knowing that they have dry, warm clothes buried in their pack.

Waterproof stuff sacks. The way to keep dry clothes that way is to use waterproof stuff sacks. Gore-Tex sacks are available, but coated nylon is cheaper. Besides, your clothes don't need to breathe in the pack, so why pay for Gore-Tex? Use different-colored sacks so you can easily identify where your gear is stashed. If you don't have waterproof stuff sacks, line the ones you do have with garbage bags.

Pack for wet weather. Normally, hikers put the sleeping bag at the bottom of their pack. But if you know you're in for a cloudburst, make sure your tent is the most accessible piece of equipment, after the things you'll be using during the day. If your pack has a separate, accessible bottom compartment, try having your tent body and your sleeping bag trade places. This way, the sleeping bag is protected in the middle of your pack, and the tent is on the bottom where you can get to it fast at the end of the day (and it won't drip on everything in your pack if you have to put it away wet). If that doesn't work for you, strap the tent to the outside of your pack in a waterproof sack. Why a waterproof sack when the tent's going to get wet the minute you put it up? There's no reason to have to crawl into a tent that is wet *inside*.

▲ ▲ ▲

How to Be a Backcountry Weather Forecaster
Bad Days

Horses in the sky. Mares' tails are those wispy little apostrophes that float innocently in a blue sky. They mean rain—especially when followed several hours later by a bank of low clouds. Figure 15 hours till the dousing comes.

Stars twinkling blue. This means rain because moist air absorbs light in the red and green spectra.

Glorious sunrises. They make super pictures, but soggy hiking. "Red sky in morning, shepherds take warning."

Pine cones. If their scales are pliable, it means they're absorbing moisture. Get out your rain jacket.

Hawks. Look for them circling more before a storm.

Campfire smoke. If it's hanging low to the ground, it's because of the low air pressure associated with a wet front.

The woody smell of woods. If you're noticing it all of a sudden, think rain. Wet air transmits smells more strongly, and plants give up more of their oils when the humidity climbs above about 80 percent.

Birds hanging out on the ground. They're just following their food supply. Before a storm, the low air pressure keeps insects low.

Ring around the moon. This is more accurately called a corona. If it's expanding, wet weather is ahead.

Swirling winds. Tree leaves turned bottom side up are a sure sign of a storm front.

Good Days

Glorious sunsets. "Red sky at night, shepherds delight." Get out your camera and sleep under the stars.

Morning mist. If it rises like it's supposed to, the day is off to a good start.

Dew. Lots of it means a fair day.

Birds flying high. Again, this is a function of air pressure. The bugs are more likely to be up high, so that's where the birds go.

Winds. Cold, fresh winds, especially when they blow in after rain and are accompanied by a dramatic temperature drop, signify a cold, dry front.

Self-locking bags. You can find a thousand reasons to admire the old-time explorers—Lewis and Clark, John Wesley Powell, John Charles Frémont, and company—but one of the most compelling is that they did it all without resealable plastic bags. Self-locking plastic bags keep everything dry, from your food supplies to your journal, your matches, camera, first-aid kit, guidebook, maps, and firestarter—among other things.

Walking wet. Don't try to out-tough the weather. In hot climates, it can be pleasant to walk in the rain without rain gear, but if you start feeling cold, it's time to gear up. Keep a slow, steady pace. You don't want to overheat.

Be prepared. In high, exposed mountains, *always* have an extra layer of clothes available where you can get to them fast in case of a sudden change in the weather. It is by no means unusual to climb to a pass on the bright sunny side of the mountain and then descend into swirling mist and wind.

Be flexible. In intermittent wet weather, take advantage of dry stretches to eat and drink—regardless of whether it's your usual time to stop for a break. You're burning a lot of calories walking and staying warm, and you need to replenish them.

A garbage bag can be used as emergency rain protection for your pack—or for you. (Photo: Jeff Scher © ERG)

Ventilate. Check to see if your rain gear has "pit zips." If so, regulate your temperature by opening or closing them.

Windshield wipers. Water-speckled glasses are a major nuisance on a rainy day. Wear a baseball cap or—even better, because it's waterproof—a plastic visor under the hood of your rain jacket to keep water off your glasses. Another choice: a rain hat with a big brim.

Dry feet in wet weather. To keep your feet dry, put on your rain pants. If your rain pants fit correctly, they extend down over your boot tops. Instead of dribbling down your legs into your boots, rain runs down the pants to the waterproof outsides of the boots. If it's too warm for rain pants, use gaiters, which will keep your feet dry for a while. Rain pants actually work better in a really foul storm because they direct the flow of water droplets away from the inside of your boots. With gaiters, water can sneak in between your skin and the fabric.

Beware of the after-rain. When the sun comes out, keep your pack cover and gaiters on (and your rain gear, too, if it's cold). Trees will be dribbling rain down onto you for several hours after the rain has stopped, especially if there's wind, and wet knee-brushing vegetation can soak feet in minutes.

Take sunshine breaks. If you're traveling through a few days of wet weather, take breaks when the sun shines and air out your gear—

After the rain stops and the sun comes out, pause to air out your gear and let it dry. (Photo: ©Karen Berger/Daniel R. Smith)

even if it didn't seem that bad when you put it away. You'll be surprised at how wet your stuff really is.

Keep snacks handy. Keep a stash of goodies in a waistpouch or somewhere else where you don't have to take off your rain cover, open your pack, and expose your gear to the weather every time you want a snack.

▲ ▲ ▲

Essential Item: Rain Gear

Why do you need it? Check out the following scenario: You are an experienced hiker on a 500-mile trip in northern Arizona. It is the last day of June. Temperatures have ranged from 70 to 120 degrees, with no precipitation. Some friends arrive to pick you up and you throw your pack in their van, opting to day hike the last few miles of your trip. Your friends drive off. You start walking, marveling at how the mileage flies by without that 30 pounds on your back. Clouds roll in. The temperature drops. It rains—hard. You start thinking about your rain gear, which is in the van. The wind picks up. You walk faster. When you get to the agreed meeting place, you notice that the back road the van must take looks too rutted for a vehicle without four-wheel drive. You start to shiver. You wonder why it is that you must learn the same lesson over and over and over again.

It rains in deserts. It rains when the meteorologist predicts sun. It rains when everyone says it's not supposed to. It rains during drought. Not often, but it only takes getting caught once to make you understand why rain gear gets a spot on the Ten Essentials list.

▬

Emergency gloves. Plastic bags, grocery bags, stuff sacks, or socks can all be used to protect your hands when a surprise cold front rolls through.

Wear wet socks. If, despite gaiters and rain pants, you still end up with wet socks at the end of the day, wring them out and, if your tent allows you to rig a clothesline, hang them up where escaping body heat will dry them out—at least a little. If the next day is sunny, wear your spare socks and hang the wet ones on your pack to finish drying. But if it's still raining, put those same horrible, wet, smelly socks back on your feet. It feels awful for about 2 minutes, but after a few minutes of walking, your feet will warm up and feel comfortable—if a little soggy. Most importantly—you'll still have nice dry socks for camp, when you stop walking and can chill more easily.

CAMPING IN THE RAIN

Protect your gear. Make sure your pack stays covered while you are setting up your tent. Work slowly and deliberately, especially in quickly deteriorating weather, to avoid dumping dry gear into puddles. Use your pack cover. If stray gear insists on spilling out (or if you're one of those hikers who packs like a traveling tinker, with stray equipment strapped all over the place), use your ground cloth to protect your stuff while you're getting the tent up. Once your tent is pitched, throw your gear inside and then slide the ground cloth underneath the tent where it belongs.

Ground-cloth basics. Double-check the ground cloth after you've put up the tent to make sure it isn't sticking out from under the tent. An improperly arranged ground cloth can act as a funnel to bring water under your tent.

Stake out! Most leaky tents aren't really leaky—they're just poorly pitched. The guy lines not only anchor the tent securely, they also stretch out the fabric so the tent sheds water properly.

Protect your sleeping bag. As soon as your tent is up and your air mattress is out, move the stuff sack with your sleeping bag into the tent. But don't take it out of its waterproof sack! You've got lots of wet clothes to deal with, not to mention your dripping-wet rain gear. Until you're all set up, keep your sleeping bag in its sack down near the foot of the tent where it's out of harm's (and water's) way.

Another use for garbage bags. Use extra garbage bags to isolate things that are already soaking-wet from your dry gear. Candidates include rain gear and stuff sacks that were riding outside your pack.

Hang a line. If you're carrying a large tent with some head room, hang a clothesline. Your body heat will help damp gear to dry.

▲ ▲ ▲

Garbage Bags

Garbage bags weigh next to nothing and have tons of uses, especially in bad weather, so take a couple of extra.

- Line regular stuff sacks with garbage bags for two layers of protection.
- Line the main compartment of your pack with a garbage bag.
- Use a garbage bag as a rain cover for your pack.
- Use a garbage bag to make a "floor" in your vestibule and keep mud and water away from your gear.
- If it's cold enough that you have to sleep with your boots, put them in a garbage bag.
- If you're caught in dangerous weather, use garbage bags as an extra layer; "wear" one by poking holes for your head and arms.
- Use a garbage bag as a place in which to stash wet gear so that everything else doesn't get soaked.
- Use a garbage bag to collect snow you'll melt for drinking water.

LIGHTNING

Know the local weather patterns. In many alpine areas, storms roll in during the afternoon, by which time you should be safely below tree line somewhere.

Ground current. Lightning moves from air to ground, and along the ground as well. To protect yourself from ground current, crouch on a coil of rope or a mattress pad. And ditch anything metal, including an external-frame pack, a steel ice ax, or aluminum ski poles.

When shelter isn't shelter. Beware of lone high trees, big rock outcroppings, and caves. Caves are not shelter from lightning; they are a lightning conduit.

One Mississippi, two Mississippi. Count the Mississippis between sighting lightning and hearing thunder, and divide by five: That's how many miles away the center of the storm is. You can also figure out if it's coming your way, retreating, or (maybe most frightening of all) circling around you.

COLD-WEATHER BACKPACKING

Windproofing your campsite. Avoid low-lying valleys where cold air settles. Gaining as little as 10 or 15 feet of elevation can make a noticeable difference. Similarly, avoid ridges, where there is no protection, and passes, which act as wind tunnels. Look for natural windbreaks like groves of trees or huge rocks or man-made shelter such as redoubts, or make your own by building a snow wall.

Snow on the roof. Four-season tents are designed to shed snow. If you're going on a trip that may or may not involve snow, your three-season tent might be okay, although if it's one of those super-ventilated ones consisting of equal parts mosquito netting and tent fabric, you could be inundated with spindrift. Another three-season tent problem: Some of them are too flat-topped to shed snow, so you'll have to knock it off. And you do have to take care of this, because the weight of a heavy dump of snow can snap your tent poles.

Open the windows. Yup, even in the snow. Without adequate ventilation, water vapor from respiration and sweat condenses and "snows" on you the next morning.

Fluff it up! When you take your sleeping bag out of its stuff sack, fluff it up by giving it a couple of good shakes. Shake it again just before you crawl in. The bag insulates by means of trapping warm air, and the fluffier it is, the more air it can trap.

Things that freeze in the night. Murphy's Law applies to the woods: Anything that can freeze, will—including boots and sweat-soaked clothing. Cram all freezables into your tent. Some other things that need a warm night's sleep include your stove and fuel bottle (they don't freeze, but they work better when warm) and anything battery-operated.

Sleep with your boots. Put your boots in a garbage bag and stuff them down at the bottom of your sleeping bag. If you don't have a garbage bag, use a stuff sack turned inside out.

Frozen boots. If your boots are frozen in the morning, try putting a bottle filled with hot water inside them. The heat will warm and soften the frozen leather around the ankles, allowing you to put the

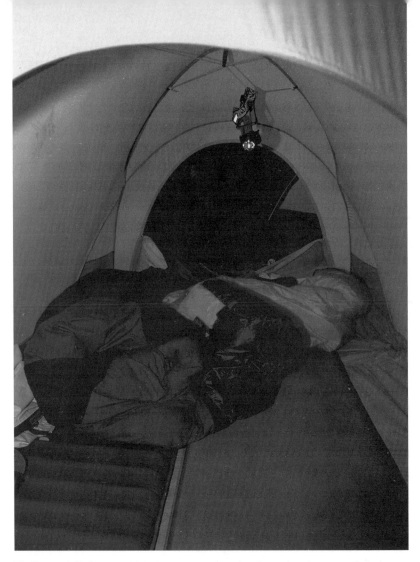

Fluff it up! Before getting into your sleeping bag, give it a good shake and be sure it's fluffed to its maximum loft. (Photo: Jeff Scher ©ERG)

boots on. But it won't defreeze the toe area. If you have an extra chemical warming pad, use it to warm the toe area. In either case, wear your camp shoes or booties to do your morning chores, and put the boots on about 5 minutes before you intend to walk. That should be enough time for your body heat to defreeze the toe area. More than 5 minutes standing around in a frozen boot, and you might find that, rather than the foot defreezing the boot, the boot is freezing the foot.

Zipping made easy. Before heading out into the winter wonderland, put leather, lanyard, or cord zipper pulls on the zippers of all your outdoor equipment. Zipper pulls can help you get zippers open with mittens on.

Sunglasses. These are one of the most important pieces of winter equipment. Even if you're not heading into snowy climes, the harsh glare of winter light is painful to stare at for long.

Sunscreen. Remember, even at low elevations, you're more exposed in winter. You can't hide from the sun beneath the foliage.

Shovel and avalanche beacons. These are essential pieces of winter gear if you're traveling in avalanche country. Take a course in avalanche safety if your backcountry peregrinations are heading in this direction. It could save your life.

▲ ▲ ▲

Essential Items: Sunglasses and Sunscreen

Why do you need them? You might scratch your head over why these get a spot on the Ten Essentials list. After all, we're talking about emergency supplies, not a Caribbean vacation, right? Wrong. If you've ever been in alpine snow walking into direct sunlight, you know why. Too much sun can cause snowblindness, a temporary but extremely painful condition. Cheap plastic lenses do not do the trick. You need sunglasses that filter out ultraviolet (UV) light. In serious conditions (snow above tree line), get glacier glasses with those leather flaps that keep light from getting in through the sides. If you're stuck without the side flaps, tape a piece of cardboard to the sides of your glasses.

As for the sunscreen, skin cancer is no joke, and a bad sunburn can ruin your trip.

STAYING WARM

Stay dry. Change into dry clothes and add extra layers immediately when you reach camp, before you start to feel cold. You start losing body heat the minute you stop hiking.

Wear nylon overlayers. Fluffy fleece attracts fresh, dry powder. The trouble starts when you wear a snow-dusted fleece jacket into your tent and all that harmless powder drips into a puddle under your sleeping bag. But snow doesn't stick to Gore-Tex or nylon, and you can shed these layers as you enter the tent. If you do a lot of winter camping, check out newer fleece garments that have a smoother finish on the outside.

Add a hot drink. Just before you crawl in for the night, treat yourself to a hot drink. Leftovers can do double duty as a hot water bottle.

Sleeping warm. It's an old Boy Scout myth that sleeping naked in a sleeping bag keeps you warmer than sleeping in clothes. This is both counterintuitive and complete nonsense. If you wake up cold, put on a hat. If you're still cold, start adding layers. If you're *still* cold, put on your rain jacket (if it's dry, of course).

Extra blankets. Okay, maybe not blankets. But fleece liners, VBLs (vapor barrier liners), and bivvys are lightweight pieces of gear that add several degrees of warmth. In real deep-freeze temperatures, some people take along a second lightweight summer sleeping bag.

Compression sacks. How do you fit all that stuff into your pack? Compression sacks have webbing that tightens down your load. You can even make your own by stitching webbing to a stuff sack and attaching plastic closures (see Figure 6).

Sleeping-bag aerobics. Isometric exercises like pressing your palms together or tensing and releasing different muscle groups can help make you warm.

A sleeping bag made for two. Zip-together bags are a fair-weather pleasure. When the thermometer really drops, couples lose too much heat from around the shoulders and neck. A water bottle will keep you warmer than your honey.

Cold feet. Make sure you're wearing dry socks. If your socks are a little

Figure 6. Make your own compression sack by sewing four pairs of webbing straps (only two pairs are shown here; the other two are on the back) and adding plastic buckles.

damp, don't just add another layer over them—change them. Take off
your sweaty liners, too.

Don't overheat. Too many layers make you sweat. How many
layers should you wear? If you're comfortable standing still, you'll be
too warm when you start to walk.

▲ ▲ ▲

Essential Item: Extra Clothing

Why do you need it? You'll appreciate that extra layer if you
soak your T-shirt with sweat and a cool wind comes up, if the
temperature at the top of the mountain is 20 degrees colder
than at the bottom, if a storm rolls in, or if you must spend a
night out unexpectedly. Day hikers need extra clothing even
more than backpackers, who, after all, usually carry tents and
stoves and sleeping bags. An important clothing hint that'll
keep you out of trouble:

Avoid cotton. Among experienced backpackers and mountaineers, cotton is referred to as "dead man's clothing." Cotton
absorbs water, and water sucks heat away from the body. Yes,
cotton feels nice. Yes, it is a nonsynthetic fabric (but often
farmed in a chemical-intensive, soil-depleting way). Nonetheless, there is no argument about this among knowledgeable
outdoorspeople: Cotton kills.

Use your head. Your hat is the next best thing to a thermostat.
Use it as your first line of defense against cold. If you don't have a hat
(an inexcusable omission!), wrap an extra piece of clothing around your
head and neck, or put on your rain jacket and pull up the hood. If
you're really cold, add layers: a balaclava, a hat, *and* a hood. Keeping
your head and neck covered will do more to keep the rest of your body
warm than a closetful of fleece.

Breathing cold air. In very cold temperatures, breathing can be
painful. A condition known as "frozen lungs" occurs when you need
more air than your respiratory system can warm. Rest often so you
don't have to gasp, and when the air is really cold, try breathing through
a scarf or face mask.

Nose. A small scrap of wool with strings pinned or sewn on can help with cold-weather breathing—and help prevent a frostbitten nose, as well. Put the piece of wool over your nose and tie the strings behind your head.

▲ ▲ ▲

Things You Have that Can Make You Warm

- Your foam pad: Sit on it to prevent loss of body heat to the cold ground.
- Plastic grocery bags: Stick them under your gloves or socks to warm up your hands or feet.
- Extra socks: If you don't have gloves, wear socks on your hands.
- Your stove: Cook up a hot drink.
- Hot water left over from dinner: Don't throw out your spaghetti water; toss in a bouillon cube and drink it when you're in your sleeping bag. If there's any left over, use it as a hot water bottle.
- Your rain gear: If it's dry, it counts as a layer, and it will keep out the wind and hold in lots of heat.
- Your tent: If you're cold while sleeping in a shelter or cabin, put up your tent for an added few degrees of warmth.
- A hat: It's the most versatile piece of extra clothing you can carry. It's vital for staying warm (and a brimmed hat in summer is sun and bug protection for your head, neck, face, and eyes).

Feet. VBLs (vapor barrier liners) can help your feet stay warm. The VBLs go over your sock liners but under your socks. They don't exactly keep your feet dry (the sweat can't escape) but they do help keep them warm. If you're not carrying VBLs, try plastic bags. Grocery store bags fit most people's feet with room to spare.

Hands. In an emergency, your extra socks can be pressed into service as rather unwieldy but serviceable gloves. Use thin polypropylene glove liners for camp chores where you need finger dexterity (pack two pairs, because they burn easily and are easy to lose).

Neck. Balaclavas, neck gaiters, and scarves are all good solutions. Lacking one of them, wrap any spare clothing around your neck.

HOT-WEATHER BACKPACKING

Hike early and late. Early means really early: 3:30 A.M. is not an unreasonable time to wake up if you want to avoid a broiling desert sun. You should be walking at first light. Then stop for a 4-hour siesta in the middle of the day, and hike again toward evening.

Use your head, part two. Just like in cold weather, a hat is your first line of defense. Wear a lightweight, breathable hat with a brim to protect your eyes. If you don't have one, try a bandanna tied around your head pirate-style. Light colors are much cooler than dark. On a really hot day, try soaking a bandanna in cold water and sticking it under your hat. You can also tuck the bandanna under your hat and let it hang down to protect your neck.

Prevent exposure. Wear loose-fitting, well-ventilated clothes. Long sleeves and long pants protect your skin from a dry, hot sun, but in hot humid weather, you may find them uncomfortably warm. Some hikers prefer cotton for desert conditions; others use synthetic fabrics that wick away sweat. Covering up not only protects you from the sun, it helps you retain water.

Other quick cool-offs. Put a cool bandanna against your face and the veins in your neck and wrists. The relief is short-lived but on a really hot day, anything helps.

Have a cold one. Keep cold drinks cold by stashing them in the middle of your pack, by wrapping them up in your sleeping pad, or by wrapping them in a piece of a foam pad, which works best. If you carry a plastic bottle of cold drink wrapped in foam pad outside your pack, make sure the pad is strapped on securely. Check it after every rest stop—and don't sit on it when you take breaks!

Make shade. If you're especially sensitive to the sun, consider an umbrella. Sounds like something you'd never do, right? Just wait till some sweltering, sun-blazing day when you're hiking over heat-reflecting rocks that look and feel like sauna stones, and you run into a fellow trekker calmly enjoying a 3-foot circle of shade! You don't have to carry the umbrella in your hand; rig it up to your pack with a hose clamp.

These hikers in Nepal are using an umbrella for a sunshade. (Photo: ©Karen Berger/Daniel R. Smith)

Portable shade. If the sun is at your back, you can create shade to protect the backs of your legs during the hottest part of the day. Tie a shirt to the bottom of the back of your pack and let it hang down and cast a shadow on your legs.

Mad dogs, Englishmen, and hikers, too. If you find yourself out in the noonday sun, use your ground cloth or a tarp to make shade. A combination of hiking sticks, grommets, and cord should do the trick. Don't bother pitching your tent; the sun shines right through the fabric (and destroys it in the process). Also remember that if your siesta is a long, drawn-out affair, the sun is going to be moving (and your shade, too) throughout the afternoon.

Hike northbound. In very sunny, exposed climates, plan your hikes going generally northbound to avoid staring into the sun all day. This is especially helpful in the winter, when the sun hangs low and fierce.

Develop a drinking habit. The most important thing you can do is drink water at every opportunity. The subject of finding, treating, and drinking water is so important that it gets its own chapter: chapter 8.

Take breaks to air out your feet. Shake your boots to remove any seeds, grains of sand, or bits of dirt that could cause blisters. (Photo: ©Karen Berger/Daniel R. Smith)

CHAPTER 7

HEALTHY HIKER

Dealing with Bumps, Bites, and Blisters

IF YOU'VE EVER given (or attended) slide shows about travel in the wilderness, you know that travelers of the armchair persuasion have a set of standard questions. At the top of the list are issues of health and safety. It seems that in the minds of most people, the outdoors is a pretty dangerous place, harboring hazards like guns, criminals, and wild animals—big ones like bears and mountain lions, and little ones like snakes and scorpions. Not to mention lightning, blizzards, and avalanches.

And yes, inherent dangers lurk when you walk away from the safety net of civilization. Every year, people die in the backcountry.

But despite the dramatic-sounding dangers, the fact is that the outdoors is one of the safest places you can be—provided that you've got a little bit of know-how and a lot of common sense. Most backcountry injuries are the collusion of bad planning and bad luck, and are entirely avoidable. A Grand Teton National Park study concluded that out of 500 incidents that required search and rescue, 499 were preventable—mostly by common sense, foresight, and the right gear. And a 1993 medical study that discussed the health of long-distance backpackers found dozens of small problems like blisters, aches and pains, and gastrointestinal complaints—but no bear maulings, no gunshot wounds, and no lightning strikes.

True, big wild animals and horrendous storms are out there. But it's the unsensational annoyances that are most likely to crimp your wilderness adventure, not the brutal indifference of an implacable universe. Away from help, small problems like bugs, a rash, or a gimpy knee can mutate into major problems, which can then be exacerbated by backcountry conditions like foul weather and dirt.

This chapter focuses on the minor problems that are the real health issues most backpackers face. It talks a lot about prevention, because prevention is by far the best cure. And it makes two assumptions: First, you have basic backcountry sense; that is, you respect the terrain in which you propose to travel and you understand that nature is tougher than you are. Second, you are reasonably competent in first aid; you've taken a course at some point in the memorable past and you can remember (at the very least) how to stop bleeding, perform artificial respiration, administer cardiopulmonary resuscitation (CPR), and treat shock. The fact that this book doesn't focus on these standard first-aid techniques doesn't means these skills aren't vital to a healthy backcountry experience; they are. But this book isn't the place to learn about them. If you haven't taken first aid, enroll in a course before you put yourself beyond the reach of telephones, roads, and 911.

▲ ▲ ▲

Medical Myths

Myth: Tourniquets stop bleeding.
Reality: Tourniquets stop bleeding so effectively that using them can lead to amputation.

Myth: A stiff drink will warm you up.
Reality: With all due apologies to St. Bernard dogs and their famous flasks, truth is, liquor dilates blood vessels—and contributes to hypothermia.

Myth: Treat a burn with butter.
Reality: Butter smothers the skin and doesn't let it breathe. Treat first- and second-degree burns with cold water.

Myth: Cut and suck a snakebite.
Reality: This can contribute to infection and spread the venom—and is unlikely to do any good. See Snakebite: Treatment, in this chapter.

Myth: Soak sprains in warm water.
Reality: For the first 24 hours after a sprain, treating with heat only increases inflammation and swelling. Use cold water. Remember the acronym RICE: rest, ice, compression, elevation.

Myth: Fast-running water is safe to drink.
Reality: Wrong again. Fast-running water fed by a beaver pond is just as likely to harbor *Giardia* as the beaver pond itself.

Myth: Climb naked into a sleeping bag with a hypothermia victim to warm him or her up.
Reality: Talk about killing with kindness! (See Hypothermia: Treatment, in this chapter). Instead, bundle the victim up in a sleeping bag. If he or she is conscious, administer hot fluids. If not, put a warm water bottle against the groin or armpits where it will warm the victim's blood without sending him or her into shock.

THE FIRST-AID KIT

The first thing to know about the perfect first-aid kit is that it doesn't exist. A 1-pound medical kit can't possibly contain the perfect solution for everything that *can* go wrong in the woods. But if you have basic first-aid skills, some standard supplies, and the ability to improvise, you can fix a lot of problems.

Check the medicine cabinet. First-aid kits tend to "lose" components over time; maybe you used a couple of Band-Aids and forgot to replenish them. Or the last time you had a cold at home, you rifled the medicines in your hiking first-aid kit rather than going out to the drugstore. Or maybe you jettisoned your hay-fever medicine on your last winter hike. Keep a list of first-aid supplies, and check it before every trip.

▲ ▲ ▲

Essential Item: First-Aid Kit

Why do you need it? This should be self-explanatory; if you need convincing, read this chapter carefully.

But you can't just run out and buy a first-aid kit, throw it in your pack, and consider yourself equipped. Trouble is, a first-aid kit rarely does much good without the knowledge to use it. So first things first; take a basic first-aid class with the American Red Cross to learn about stopping bleeding, treating burns, performing mouth-to-mouth resuscitation, and other basics. Then take a wilderness first-aid class to learn how to apply these skills in a wilderness setting.

There are also several lightweight wilderness first-aid books on the market designed to be of minimum burden to a pack weight–conscious backpacker.

Protect adhesives and keep them clean. Adhesive first-aid products such as Band-Aids, bandages, moleskin, and medicine tape need to be protected from moisture, or over time they stop sticking. Store them in plastic resealable bags.

Freshen up supplies. Even carefully packed supplies have a limited shelf life—especially when part of that life is spent in the woods. If you've taken your first-aid kit out on several trips, be sure to check that the products are still good. It's better to splurge a few pennies on new moleskin than to find out that you can't treat a blister because the adhesive deteriorated.

Use a commercial backcountry first-aid kit. Sure, you'll have to modify it. Maybe you need a knee brace, allergy medicine, or a bee-sting kit, and those things aren't included. Maybe you don't need all those different sizes of gauze bandages, or you prefer Tylenol to ibuprofen (or vice versa, or neither of them). Maybe you find the thought of using one of those miniature Band-Aids in the woods ridiculous. Regardless, a commercial first-aid kit contains most necessities, and even if you don't use every single item, a commercial kit is more economical than purchasing all the components individually. Plus, it will get you thinking about what you need and what you don't need. One thing you might do without: the case the stuff comes in. For most short trips, a self-locking plastic bag will do; it weighs less and provides better protection against water.

BLISTERS: PREVENTION

Boots that fit. Preventing blisters starts when you buy a pair of boots. Three major keys to a good fit: The toe box is roomy enough to wiggle your toes, you don't feel your toes banging against the leather when you stub your toes or when you walk down a ramp, and the heels have just enough room that if you push your foot toward the front of your boot, you can squeeze a finger behind your heel. But your heel shouldn't slip up and down as you walk.

Compare new boots to old boots. A new boot feels stiffer and tighter than a broken-in old boot. But bring along a pair of really comfortable old hiking boots, outdoor shoes, or work boots to compare the new boots to. If the boot you're trying on feels a *lot* different, keep looking.

Buy boots in the afternoon. Your feet swell in the afternoon, so that's when you should try on boots.

Match socks to boots. Various thicknesses of socks are available, and the thickness you choose will influence the fit of the boot. Cushy socks can make a big difference, especially on rocky, hard terrain. Just be sure to try on boots wearing the kind of socks you plan to use.

Insoles. Insoles are available in a variety of shapes and sizes: half inserts for the front of the foot, inserts for just the heel, orthotics, squishy gel-filled inserts, cushioned inserts that promise you'll feel like a cloud walker. The insoles that come with most boots are cheap and thin. If you plan to use thicker ones (and they can add quite a measure of comfort), those are what you should wear when trying on the boots.

Break in your boots. This is true of even lightweight boots. It doesn't matter what the manufacturer says about whether the boots need to be broken in; they do. Your feet and the boots have to get to know each other, and this is far more happily accomplished without a pack on. You don't want to discover fit or blister problems in the back-of-beyond. I always put 50 miles of local walking on a pair of new boots before I head out. And I don't get blisters.

Know your feet. Most people have areas that are especially prone to blistering. Pretreat such problem spots. Also, most people have feet that are slightly different in size. If the difference is noticeable, vary the socks and insoles to customize the fit for each foot.

Lacing tricks. Some fitting problems can be solved by anchoring your foot more securely in one part of the boot but not the other. Triple twisting or half-knotting the laces over the arch makes it possible to vary the tightness of the front and back of the boot. You can tighten up the toe area but leave the arch and heel a little looser. Or, you can give yourself a little more room in the front of the boot by loosening up the laces over the toes, knotting at the arch, and then tightening up around the ankle. See Figure 7.

Padding the boot. In the field, try using strips of moleskin to take up space in a too-big boot, or to cover up a seam or protrusion that is irritating your skin.

Have a pedicure. At least clip your toenails. This is the first thing to do if you're starting to get little blisters on the sides of your toes. If, after being

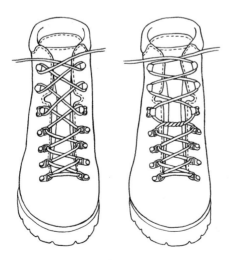

Figure 7. Lacing tricks: At left the laces are looped over the top of the hooks so they are less likely to loosen as you walk; at right, the triple twist lets you vary the tightness of the laces over the foot and around the ankle.

clipped, the nail is still digging into an adjacent toe, wrap a piece of tape around the offending nail, the blistering toe, or both.

Stretch the toe box. A time-honored way to break in boots to your feet is to soak them wet and walk them dry. Wrap blister-prone areas of your feet in moleskin before you do this, because wet feet blister readily. After the dousing, put on dry socks. Note: Some experts disagree, saying that immersion in water isn't good for the leather. That may be, but it makes me wonder: What do those folks do when it rains for a week? After the boots dry, treat them with a leather conditioner.

Sock liners. Wear liners made of a wicking material like Thermax or polypropylene, which move the sweat away from your feet. Do not wear cotton or cotton-blend socks. Cotton absorbs several times its weight in water and holds the water close to your skin, where it causes blisters. This is a promise.

Outer socks. These should be medium-weight wool, perhaps with some synthetic content to maintain their shape and add strength (100 percent wool ragg socks tend to wear out faster than 80-20 blends). Special hiking socks have thicker soles for cushioning your feet. It's a small difference, but after tens of thousands of steps in a day, that small difference adds up.

Put on dry socks at lunch. When you're walking along on a warm day, your feet might feel pretty comfortable. You'll be surprised to find out how sweaty and damp they really are. At longer rest breaks like lunchtime, take the time to air out your feet—and your socks. Or put on a dry pair.

Air your socks. In camp, check your socks for grass seeds, grains of sand, dirt, and stuck-on pine sap, which can harden and cause blisters. After you've picked out the prickles, air out the socks. It makes a difference when you're wearing the same socks several days in a row.

Do the laundry. Take advantage of dry weather and rinse sock liners as soon as you get into camp (they take longer to dry than you might think, and a couple of hours of sunshine can make a great deal of difference). If the liners are still wet in the morning, wear a pair of spares and hang the wet ones on the back of your pack to dry. Be sure you tie them securely: Socks can snag on branches overhanging the trail.

Baby your feet. Stick them in a stream. Wash and dry them. Shake on some medicated foot powder. Give yourself a foot massage. Better yet, trade foot rubs with an accommodating hiking partner. Massage promotes the flow of blood through your feet and helps to flush out lactic acids that are the by-product of muscular activity. But who cares about that? A foot massage just feels great!

Wear running shoes. On easy terrain in reasonably dry weather, especially if you're going out for just a couple of days (so you're not carrying tons of food weight), you may not even need boots. This is a personal choice: Some people want the ankle support of heavier-weight boots for all hikes. If you're wearing boots, consider carrying a pair of camp shoes for evening comfort. If those camp shoes are running shoes, remember that you can slip them on to hike in if your boots are causing blister problems.

▲ ▲ ▲

Hot Spots

You took care to make sure your boots really fit when you bought them. You broke them in before your hike. But in the field, they just don't feel right.

- If you need more room, cut out a piece of the insole.
- If part of the boot is too loose, you can take up some space by inserting a thicker insole (you might have one in your camp shoes, if they are running shoes).
- Stick some moleskin inside your boot to take up extra space.
- If a seam or protrusion in your boot is rubbing, tape over it with duct tape.
- Wear a thicker (or thinner) sock to fine-tune the fit.

BLISTERS: TREATMENT

Stop immediately. The second you feel something pinching, rubbing, or otherwise bothering your foot, *stop!* Right that exact, very minute. Most serious blisters—the ones that make your feet look like raw hamburger—are due to violating this extremely simple principle. You ignore

Stop immediately if you feel a hot spot. (Photo: ©Jeff Scher)

the pain because you're tough. You keep going because it's not that far to camp. You're not a wimp. Okay, have it your way: hamburger feet.

Locate the problem. Most often, the problem is something minor that can be fixed, say, a speck of dirt digging into sweaty skin or a bunched-up sock. If the problem is your boot, rub the inside of it with the round part of a closed pocket knife or a small round stone. This simple, quick fix can give you just that extra millimeter of room.

Treating a blister means it won't get worse—and possibly ruin your hike. (Photos: ©Jeff Scher)

Let sweaty feet dry. Sometimes blistering is caused by sweaty feet sliding around in too-stiff boots. Another cause of sweating is wearing gaiters (even Gore-Tex gaiters) on a hot day. Let sweaty feet dry before you put adhesive treatments like moleskin on them, because adhesives don't adhere well to wet skin.

Protect the area. A small red spot caused by a grain of sand that you've found and removed might just need a Band-Aid. A more angry-looking spot might require additional padding, say, a layer of moleskin. It's best to put the moleskin over the Band-Aid so that the adhesive doesn't stick to the tender area. You don't want to compound the problem when you remove the dressing.

To pierce or not to pierce. If you've already got a blister, go ahead and pierce it. There's some controversy about this, but in the backcountry, the blister is likely to burst because of continuing pressure on the area, so you might as well pierce it yourself when you can at least try to ensure clean conditions. Use a sterile needle (hold it to a lit match, then douse it in alcohol). Clean the blister with a dab of alcohol, pierce it, put some antibiotic ointment on it for good measure, and cover it with a dressing.

Dressings. The best blister remedy I know is a product by Spenco called Second Skin. This dressing takes pressure off the blister and relieves pain. It's interesting that the product was originally developed as a treatment for burns—because blisters are, after all, nothing more than friction burns. Put the squishy gel directly on the blister and cover it up with medicine tape.

MUSCULOSKELETAL PROBLEMS: PREVENTION

This category is home to all the cranky muscles and squeaky knees and achy ankles that accompany a not-quite-as-fit-as-it-should-be body through the wilderness. (Note: Fitness fanatics aren't immune. If they carry too much weight and hike too many miles, they too can suffer from all the aches and pains their less-fit hiking brethren are subject to.) The kinds of problems you'll encounter depend on a whole slew of factors: your fitness, your age, the length and difficulty of your hike, your daily mileage, and your pack weight—to start. For shorter hikes, cranky muscles are likely to be the main complaint. For longer adventures, knee and joint problems can develop after many miles of steep ups and downs.

Fitness is key. The amount of outdoor aching you endure is directly proportional to how often you opted for a doughnut over a salad and a couch over a Stairmaster in the weeks before your hike. A combination of a healthy diet with strength training, aerobic exercise, and stretching helps get you ready to climb big mountains carrying a heavy pack. (It's also not a bad formula for living a healthy life.) Pay particular attention to developing your quadriceps muscles, which not only help you power up big hills, but help you get down without blowing out your knees.

Know your limits. Start slowly! Walking 8 miles on city streets might take you no more than 2½ hours. Carrying a full pack 8 miles uphill can take you most of a day and leave you exhausted at the end of it. Don't underestimate the demands of backpacking—or overestimate your fitness. When you're planning a hike, look at the elevation gain as much as at the mileage, and figure conservatively.

Stretch. At the beginning of the day, stretch after a few minutes of walking. Standard running stretches limber up your calves, hamstrings, and quads, and a few neck and back exercises help prevent twinges caused by your pack.

Walking sticks. Along with all their other benefits, walking sticks take literally tons of stress off of knee and ankle joints, especially on steep downhills.

MUSCULOSKELETAL PROBLEMS: TREATMENT

Cut your mileage. Walking an average pace of 2 miles an hour for, say, a 7-hour day, yields a daily total of 14 miles. Doesn't sound too extreme, does it? In reality, unless you're in great shape to begin with, you'll find that it takes at least a week to break in to that kind of all-day backpacking, and 3 or 4 weeks to break in to doing really big mileage. Weekend hikers will have a happier time if they plan modest mileage, long lunch breaks, and plenty of stops for views and snacks. If you experience aches and pains, slow down and reduce your daily mileage.

Stretch. Stretching is good treatment as well as good prevention. If you find yourself stiffening up during the day (especially after breaks), stretch just before you put your pack back on.

Massage. Trade rubdowns with your hiking partner. A muscle massage of only a few minutes can do wonders for sore, overworked muscles.

Take a rest day. Take a day off in town, find a hotel with a bathtub, and let those muscles soak! Muscles that become overfatigued can lead to tendonitis, a much more serious condition.

FALLS, SPRAINS, AND STRAINS: PREVENTION

Take breaks. The most dangerous time of day is the last hour of hiking, when you're tired and may be a little careless. Pay attention to both the condition of the trail and the condition of your body; if necessary, take frequent breaks or stop to eat something before tackling that last mile-long descent down a scree field. Above all, ignore the little voice that urges you to push on because it's only another mile to camp. If you need a break, take one.

Walking sticks. Again, walking sticks make a tremendous difference on steep, rocky, unstable trails—the kind that make you hop down big steps and balance on rocks that wiggle underfoot. This is especially important for older hikers. Medical studies indicate that some loss of balance is a normal part of the aging process, starting at around the age of sixty. Hiking sticks (again, two are better than one) not only take pressure off your joints—they also help with balance and they enable you to negotiate steeper steps and tricky descents more safely.

Technique. When you start to fall, there's that seemingly endless split second when you know you've lost control and you see everything in slow motion. Once gravity takes over, the best thing to do is to relax and go with the flow. If you've lost your footing on tricky ground—say, the boulder you committed your weight to has slid underfoot and you're

Walking sticks take pressure off your joints. (Photo: ©Jeff Scher)

flailing off balance and headed for an ankle-twisting landing in a rock field—try to regain control by increasing your momentum until you are in sync with your fall, and then reining yourself back in. Huh? Practice on a balance beam a couple of inches off the ground (you'll often find low balance beams in public parks where there are exercise courses). Play around until you lose your balance, then try to regain it. Watch what you do when you're successful: You speed up your footwork. On rocks, it works the same way. If you're committed to a fall, don't try to stop. Instead, try to choreograph the next few steps. Keep your feet moving from one rock to another, pushing off and landing. Each time you hop from one foot to the other, you gain a little control until finally you are traveling at the same pace and in the same direction as the fall. That's when you regain control. Think of it as hitting an icy patch when driving your car: You don't slam on the brakes; instead, you try to regain control by riding into sync with the skid.

Extra support. Falls are sometimes caused when a weak joint or muscle refuses to do what's asked of it. This is especially true of knees. A brace can help. But use them only when muscles are fatigued, because overuse can weaken the muscles that most need strengthening. If you have an ongoing problem, consult a physician or a physical therapist, who may be able to suggest specific exercises and treatment.

FALLS, SPRAINS, AND STRAINS: TREATMENT

If in doubt, treat as a fracture. Apply a splint that immobilizes the joints above and below the injury. For a splint, use a tree branch, a walking stick (the ones that are telescopic), tent poles, or even your sleeping pad. Be sure not to cut off circulation when you apply the splint in place.

RICE. Rest, ice, compression, and elevation is the standard treatment for sprains and strains. Rest is crucial; if you've got swelling or pain, give your joints a chance to heal. How long depends on the injury. Recovery could require only a couple of days—but a more serious injury could require weeks, or even months. In a backpacker's case, ice is likely to be supplanted with cold compresses (read: bandanna dipped into cold water). Compression can be achieved with an elastic bandage (be sure not to tie it too tightly). Elevation is self-explanatory: take a load off and put the injured joint above your heart to reduce the flow of blood, which contributes to swelling.

Dislocated shoulders. In the field, you can use gravity to pop the dislocation back in place. The victim lies on something a few feet above the ground (a rock, a fallen tree log, a picnic table). The injured arm is left to dangle down, with a weight tied on. Gravity will pull the shoulder back into place.

Taping. If you've never practiced wrapping an ankle with tape, you might be surprised to learn just how effective this low-tech solution is. It can make the difference between mobility and immobility. Elastic bandages and braces are also effective on knees.

Reduce the load. Ask your hiking partners to take all of your pack weight (or, at least, as much as possible) and proceed *slowly.* If you're not using a hiking stick, try to find one. If you're using one, try to find a second one. If the injury is severe, stop for the day and make camp; further walking on a badly sprained ankle can reduce your ability to hike back out safely.

CUTS AND WOUNDS: PREVENTION

Playing with knives. This is a common-sense issue. Perhaps the most common backcountry wound is when you try to slice a piece of sausage with your pocket knife and you slice your hand instead. Be careful!

Keep knives sharp. This is counterintuitive, but true: A sharp knife is much less likely to go skittering off whatever you are trying to cut and slice your hand instead.

CUTS AND WOUNDS: TREATMENT

Clean the cut. If it's deep, stop the bleeding: Elevate the wound and, if necessary, apply direct pressure (on the cut itself). Putting pressure on the brachial or femoral arteries in the arm or groin is not very effective because collateral arteries can still supply blood to the wound. You may use such indirect pressure in conjunction with—but not instead of—direct pressure. Butterfly closures, Band-Aids, gauze bandages, or athletic tape can hold the cut closed.

Abrasions. A nasty slide down a rocky slope can leave you with shredded skin embedded with sand and dirt. Wash the wound and carefully remove as much dirt and gravel as you can. Apply an antibiotic ointment and a clean, dry bandage.

FRICTION RASHES: PREVENTION

Like a blister, chafing is the kind of nasty little irritation that usually poses no danger aside from abject misery. And, like a blister, it's a tricky problem to foresee or prevent; you may not even know you're prone to it, because the problem sometimes surfaces only after prolonged walking in hot, humid weather. Heavier hikers, as well as hikers with large, muscular thighs, are prime targets for between-the-legs chafing.

Another spot that can be prone to heat-related rashes is the small of your back (more commonly a problem for wearers of internal-frame packs, which ride closer to the back). You can also develop heat-friction rashes anyplace where your clothing tends to get bunched or lumpy under your pack straps, or anyplace where seams rub against skin—for instance, the elastic bands on a pair of underwear.

Test-drive clothing before your hike. Just trying it on in the store dressing room isn't enough: Make sure that it doesn't chafe and irritate you after several miles of walking with a pack on. Fixing clothing-related problems is usually no more than a question of tugging and pulling things into a new position, but you might need to replace or remove an item that gives you consistent problems. Know which parts of your body are susceptible. To prevent chafing thighs—the most common problem—try wearing extra-long shorts or bicycle shorts.

FRICTION RASHES: TREATMENT

Remove the cause. The rash is only going to get worse unless whatever is rubbing or scratching is removed. Once the irritation is stopped, these rashes heal quickly. A dash of cornstarch or petroleum jelly can alleviate the problem for a while.

Ointments. Overnight, apply an ointment like hydrocortisone to reduce inflammation.

No sweat. For pack-related problems, try wiping your sweat away with cold water several times a day.

BURNS: PREVENTION

Stoves and fires. Avoid these predictable scenarios of a burn in the making: a too-large, too-full pot on a stove that isn't entirely stable; the same pot set on unstable logs on a cook fire; careless use of matches near fuel bottles; placing the fuel tank too close to the stove; long hair dangling over a fire or stove; cooking in your tent; priming your stove in your vestibule; trying to jump-start a floundering fire by pouring a little fuel onto it.

Handling hot water. Most backpackers use pot grabbers to handle cooking chores. Be sure you have a firm grip on a pot before trying to move it or pour from it. If you're pouring hot water from pot to water bottle, or any other container, make sure the other container is sitting stably on the ground. Never try to pour hot water into a container someone is holding for you.

Hot pots. A pot set near the fire can retain heat long after you've stopped cooking.

Fire safety. Basic common sense says if you've got a fire going, you should have a supply of water on hand with which to put it out.

Sunburn. Don't wait till it's too late. Use a sunscreen with SPF (sun protection factor) of 15 or higher, especially in very exposed areas like deserts, above tree line, and in the snow. Reapply it regularly. Cover up with clothes. Don't neglect your ears, your neck, and the back of your legs.

Sunburned lips. Use a lip balm with an SPF factor and reapply it regularly. Too much exposure to the sun can bring out cold sores caused by the herpes simplex virus.

BURNS: TREATMENT

Stop, drop, and roll. If you, your hair, or your clothing catches fire, don't run—the air you fan makes the flames worse. Drop immediately to the ground and roll to smother the flames.

First- and second-degree burns. A cold-water compress can take out some of the pain and help start the healing process. In the backcountry, of course, you'll have to improvise: your bandanna soaked in cold water will do. Do not break second-degree burn blisters: After immersing in cold water, cover them with sterile bandages.

Third-degree burns. These occur when the skin is charred. These are rare in the backcountry, but they are extremely serious, probably require evacuation, and must be treated in a hospital. Do *not* put water on third-degree burns. Do not try to remove clothing that has stuck to the skin. Cover the wound with a dry dressing. Give the victim sips of water with a little sugar and salt added: This helps prevent dehydration. Treat for shock.

Sunburn. Avoid continued exposure. Cover up with clothing and apply a sunscreen with a high SPF.

BUG BITES AND STINGS: PREVENTION

Know before you go. Sometimes the path of least resistance is the path of least regrets. It's not wimpy to avoid Maine during the blackfly hatch—it's smart. Wet places are buggier than dry places; low-lying areas buggier than alpine areas—except during snowmelt. Bug populations fluctuate depending on precipitation, temperature, and humidity. Check with the locals for the current dope on bugs.

Repellents. DEET is the repellent that works the best in test after test. It's a strong chemical, though (diethyltoluamide): Store it in its own resealable bag away from plastics and coated nylons, because it can eat through them. A $3 bottle of DEET can ruin a $300 piece of equipment. If you find that image troubling (after all, the repellent is going on your skin), a natural alternative called citronella is also effective.

Pump it up! Pump sprays are a clear choice over aerosols. They're lighter to carry, easier to dispose of, and better for the environment. Pump sprays are less concentrated than the little plastic bottles of 100 percent DEET, so if you anticipate a particularly buggy hike, you might want one of each: the heavy artillery for when the going gets rough, and the pump spray for your clothing—a big advantage, because mosquitoes, blackflies, and lots of other tormentors won't let a measly T-shirt get between them and a meal. But don't spray DEET bug dope on high-tech synthetic fabrics (coated nylon, Gore-Tex, your tent). The stuff can eat through synthetics like acid. Use citronella instead.

Repellents on clothing. To minimize how much DEET you absorb through your skin, try spraying some on a bandanna and wearing it around your neck. Other places you may want to spray: your T-shirt and hat brim.

Don't smell like a flower. Avoid using lotions, scented soaps, or shampoos. An exception: Sunscreens with insect repellents don't smell half bad and solve two problems at once.

The dope on Skin-so-Soft. Here's another possible exception to the "don't smell too good" rule. This skin lotion, made by Avon, has garnered an ardent following among hardcore Northwoods types as a repellent par excellence. Field tests fail to uphold the folklore, and Avon makes no claims that its product works as an insect repellent and does not market it as such. Nonetheless, in Maine's blackfly country, you'll see tough-looking camouflage-clad outdoorspeople rubbing in the sweet-smelling lotion before heading out to the woods. These are people who know their blackflies, and they swear by the stuff.

Fabric softener sheets. I've never tried this, but some experienced hikers say it helps. One woman ties the strips to various parts of her backpack. She says she feels a little silly decked out in strips of fabric softener, but the bugs take warning and leave the area.

Bug repellent and your eyes. Avoid putting bug dope on your forehead; it'll drip into your eyes. Instead, wear a brimmed hat. It'll keep deerflies out of your hair and other flies from buzzing around your face. A dab of repellent on the brim helps protect your forehead from mosquitoes without mixing in with sweat and stinging your eyes.

Cover up. Clothing can save your sanity. White clothing appears to repel bugs, at least a little. Loose-fitting clothing is difficult for bugs to bite through.

Use a head net. You can buy one or, in the field, if the bugs are really driving you nuts, you can make your own if you carry a piece of cheesecloth. Improvise a mosquito hat by pinning the cheesecloth to your hat brim with safety pins. Keep the cheesecloth from being sucked into your mouth every time you breathe by weighing it down with a few pebbles tucked in where the "hem" would be if you were going to make a hem. Hold the pebbles in place with a rubber band.

Woodsmoke. If you've got a fire going, stand in or around the woodsmoke for a few minutes. The smell that clings to your clothes and hair repels bugs.

In blackfly country or during alpine snowmelt, a head net can keep bugs away. (Photo: Jeff Scher ©ERG)

Watch out for yellow jackets. Yellow jackets and flies are attracted to strong smells—like your socks! Hang damp and smelly clothing out to dry a little way away from you, and let the bugs swarm on them instead of on you. But give the socks a good shake when you retrieve them.

Inherit the wind. Mosquitoes can't fly in a strong wind. During bug season, choose your resting and camping places up high, in the open, where you can catch a breeze. Dry, rocky places are better than meadows.

Take a bath. Although blackflies breed in fast-running water, they tend to do their biting in the forests. If you're looking for respite, you may find it near a waterfall or along the banks of a fast-running stream.

Use a bug shelter. A tarp sounds like a great idea for dry climates when you want just-in-case-it-snows-in-June-in-Arizona protection without hauling a lot of weight around. But tarps don't keep out the bugs. A better lightweight strategy might be to take some sort of ultralight rain protection (a large ground cloth, a small tarp, or a bivvy) and a bug shelter (yes, there are such things; check at your outfitter).

Take the right sleeping bag. In summertime, many hikers take a heavier bag than they need, figuring they can just sleep on top of it when the weather gets too hot. But this can be a problem if you're sleeping under the stars, under a tarp, or in a lean-to in hot weather. You crawl out of the bag because it's 90 degrees and too hot to sleep, and you spend the rest of the night trying to ignore the fact that your unprotected body has become a bug buffet.

Watch out for scorpions. These fearsome-looking arachnids can pack a fierce, sometimes poisonous sting, but only one species, *Ceturoides sculptuates*, has a potentially fatal sting. It's found in the desert Southwest, and is a greenish yellow color, from ½ to 3 inches long. Fortunately, scorpions (unlike mosquitoes) aren't aggressive. You're most likely to encounter them hiding in your boots (always shake them out before putting them on) or sleeping bag. Wear shoes around camp and be careful collecting firewood or rocks for building a fire ring. If you are bitten, treat the sting as you would a wasp sting (see the next section).

BUG BITES AND STINGS: TREATMENT

Itching. Over-the-counter remedies like calamine lotion and hydrocortisone ointment take the itch out. You can also try a dab of rubbing alcohol or witch hazel.

Stings. Bee, wasp, and hornet stings are more serious. Basic first aid for stings is soap and water and cool compresses. An oral antihistamine can reduce the stinging and swelling.

Anaphylaxis. This is an allergic reaction to stings, leading to anaphylactic shock. If you know you are allergic, carry a prescription beesting kit, and warn your hiking partners and tell them how to help you in an emergency.

TICKS: PREVENTION

It's nothing short of gross to take off your clothes and find a bloodswollen tick having dinner on your skin. But nasty as that is, it's only the beginning of the problem. Ticks can carry potentially debilitating diseases like Lyme disease, Rocky Mountain spotted fever, and erlychiosis. I'm always suspicious of the new outdoors danger-of-the-week (it seems the media delights in the bugaboos of the backcountry). But because I spend several months each year in the woods, I see firsthand when the problem stops being something I read about in the paper and becomes something that happened to someone I know. I can count quite a number of acquaintances who have come down with Lyme disease in the last few years, so the danger is definitely in that second category.

However, to put it into perspective: I've never had a tick burrow in, and only a couple of times have I found one crawling around on me. Partly, this is avoidance. I follow some of the precautions listed below. But after 10,000 miles of hiking, I'm starting to think that maybe there isn't a tick lurking on every blade of grass waiting for hapless hikers to pass by. The conclusion? Be aware—but don't be panicked.

Know when you are in tick country. High grasses in open fields are Tick-City Central. If you go through a meadow with grasses swishing against your legs, do a quick tick-check once you get to the other side.

Check yourself. A couple of times a day is not too often. Generally, ticks take several hours to burrow in and transmit disease, so it's not like you have to catch them immediately. The deer tick is teeny, as small as a speck of dirt. Most hikers are somewhat casual about backwoods hygiene, but in tick country it pays to get rid of the dirt so you can identify the ticks.

DEET. This is by far the best tick repellent, so spray it on your lower legs, which is where ticks tend to hop on. Ticks wander over your body looking for a nice warm, moist place to snuggle in. A dab of DEET on your thighs acts as a roadblock. A little dab around your waist posts one of their favorite burrowing places out-of-bounds.

Gaiters. Gaiters protect your legs and block ticks from getting into your socks, another favorite burrowing place. Spraying repellent on your gaiters doubles the protection—use citronella if possible; DEET is too hard on the synthetic fabrics your gaiters are probably made of.

What to wear. Choose white or light-colored clothing. You can more easily spot the little blood-suckers on a light background. And wear long pants tucked into socks. Sure, it looks a little stupid, but it protects your skin and gives the ticks no place to go.

TICKS: TREATMENT

Don't panic. Not all ticks carry disease, and even those that do don't always transmit it. Remember, they need to be embedded for several hours to transmit disease.

Tick removal. The trick is to remove the tick without breaking it into pieces, leaving the head buried in your skin (which can cause infection). Trying to entice the tick away from its dinner hour isn't easy. Inconsistently effective folk remedies include smothering it in petroleum jelly (to make it come out for air) or irritating it with DEET, a dab of gasoline, or the tip of a hot match. (Hint: Your skin isn't going to care for the last alternative.) More reliable are tick extractors, which are commercially available. If the tick isn't too deeply embedded, try tweezing it out: Grip the tick as close to your skin as possible, hold it gently, and pull it straight out.

After the fact. Lyme disease sometimes announces itself several weeks after the fact by a telltale "bull's-eye" rash that occurs where the bite took place. The rash—and any other symptoms, which include fatigue, fever, and joint pain—should send you to a doctor. Be sure to tell your doctor that you've been in the woods and suspect Lyme disease.

You might want to go to a specialist familiar with the disease, because it is easy to misdiagnose.

POISONOUS PLANTS: PREVENTION

Don't underestimate the power of these pesky plants—poison ivy, poison sumac, and poison oak—all of which can cause a torturously itchy rash that lasts, in some cases, for weeks. The culprit is the substance urushiol, which some 80 percent of the population is allergic to. All parts of these plants are poisonous in all seasons.

Identification. In order to avoid them, you've got to be able to identify them. Poison sumac is a shrub or small tree (not a vine) growing in low-lying coastal areas. It has leaf clusters of seven to eleven, which look vaguely sumac-ish, although the leaves are rounder. In poison ivy and poison oak, look for leaf clusters of three. Poison ivy and poison oak can grow as shrubs or vines. They can adapt to a wide variety of environments, from New Mexico riverbeds to shady Oregon forests and sunny Pennsylvania ridges, but they don't grow in far northern latitudes or above tree line. All three plants have small white berries in the fall. See Figure 8.

Winter. All three plants are poisonous in winter as well as summer. You can identify poison ivy and poison oak by their vines. Mature vines growing on trees have wrist-thick roots that are covered with what looks like red hair. The hair is actually smaller roots, which

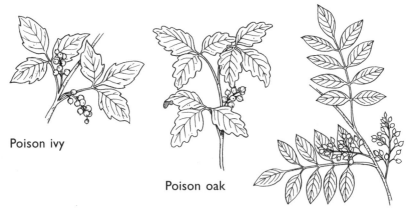

Poison ivy

Poison oak

Figure 8

Poison sumac

attach the plant to its host. Young vines have a few of the same red-dish brown hairs, but they're not nearly as dense or as obvious; you have to look for them.

Developing the allergy. Say you played in a vacant lot back when you were a kid, and everyone else got a rash from poison ivy except you. You might think you're not allergic. Think again: You can develop an allergy to urushiol over time and exposure.

Secondary contact. You don't have to come into direct contact with the plant to get the rash. Petting a dog that's taken a romp through a patch of poison ivy can have just as itchy an outcome. So can touching clothes or tools that have come into contact with it. You can also have a serious allergic reaction if you breathe in smoke from burning poisonous plants.

Wear gaiters. In poisonous plant country, wear gaiters, or—if it's really bad—rain pants. Even so, try to avoid heedless wallowing in a poison ivy patch: The oil that causes the allergic reaction has a tendency to stick around on clothing, boots, and gear.

Pre-exposure treatments. If you're highly allergic, try pre-exposure lotions, available at outfitting stores.

POISONOUS PLANTS: TREATMENT

Anti-ivy solutions. If you know, or suspect, you've been in any of the poisonous plants, you can drastically minimize its effects by washing with one of the currently available anti-ivy solutions. These solutions are heavy-duty abrasives; they're unpleasant to use, but they do the job of removing the urushiol, which is responsible for the rash. You can use these solutions anytime after exposure. If you don't realize you've been exposed and you get the beginnings of a rash, washing with these solutions can minimize your reaction.

Use cold running water. Warm water opens your skin's pores, letting in more of the offending oils. Also be careful not to spread the urushiol around when you're washing the exposed areas.

Yellow laundry soap. This is a popular remedy, although not effective for highly allergic people.

Medical remedies. If, despite all of your best efforts, you come down with a rash, you might want to pay a visit to your physician. If you are highly allergic, the rash can linger for weeks or even become systemic, where the allergic reaction gets into your bloodstream and causes rashes to spontaneously appear on unexposed parts of your body. Depending on the severity of your reaction, you may be treated with prednisone shots or pills, topical ointments, or antihistamines. With medical treatments, the rash and itching start to recede almost immediately. If you are too far in the backcountry to seek immediate treatment from a doctor, wash the rash, cover with a dry dressing to keep from exposing other body parts, and leave it completely alone. If you think your allergic reaction has gone systemic, try taking antihistamine pills. It's worth noting that few people develop this severe a reaction upon their first exposure. If you are highly allergic, talk to your doctor about getting some prescription medicine in case of a severe outbreak in the backcountry.

SNAKEBITE: PREVENTION

Identify. There are only four kinds of venomous snakes in the United States: rattlesnake (several species), cottonmouth (also called water moccasin), copperhead, and coral snake. The first three are pit vipers, identifiable by their wedge-shaped heads and the pits under their eyes. Rattlesnakes, of course, have their distinctive rattles. Copperheads have an hourglass pattern of copper-brown and gold. Water moccasins are dullish brown and extremely thick-bodied. Coral snakes are easily identified by their red, yellow, and black coloring; if the red and yellow bands are touching each other, it's a coral snake. If red and black bands are touching each other, it's not a coral snake, but one of its mimics.

Avoid. Use your hiking stick as a snake detector, especially if you're stepping among rocks and boulders in snake country. When rock scrambling, climb with your eyes: Don't put your hands where you can't see them. Step on obstacles, not over them; that way, you can check out what you're stepping into on the other side of the obstacle.

Know their habits. On a hot day, snakes hide in the shade. On a cool day, they head for sunny rocks.

Rattlesnakes. This "gentleman" snake usually gives plenty of warning. They usually are aware of you long before you become aware of them. If you've never heard a rattlesnake before, you might worry about confusing the sound of its rattle with a bird hopping among the underbrush or a buzzing insect. Don't. The sound a rattlesnake makes is instantly recognizable. Immediately take three or four big steps away from the sound (usually this means stepping backward), and then, from a safe distance, look for the snake so you can walk around it. At midday, snakes are torpid, and they may be disinclined to yield the right-of-way. If possible, detour around them. If that isn't possible, a last resort is to fight for the right-of-way by throwing rocks from a safe distance. Note: A safe distance is as far away as you can get and still throw the rock—multiple lengths of the snake's body. Use small rocks, and aim to irritate, not to kill. The point is to get the snake to move.

SNAKEBITE: TREATMENT

Don't panic! Snakebite may be the most overrated wilderness injury of them all. First, snakebites are extremely rare. Second, only about half of venomous snakes actually inject venom when they bite. And third, snakebites are almost never fatal. (Any exceptions are likely to be young children, the elderly, and people in frail health to begin with.)

Treat for shock. Keep the victim calm. Elevating the feet is standard shock treatment, and it makes sense because most backcountry snakebites are to the legs. Keep the victim's temperature stable, providing an awning of shade with your ground cloth if necessary. Make sure the victim has plenty of liquids on hand.

The truth about snakebite kits. One expert on venomous snakes calls snakebite kits "a license to kill." The old cut-and-suck treatment has been roundly and vehemently discredited; it actually helps the venom spread faster and can cause infection to boot.

Go for help. The fact is, no matter how remote the wilderness you're in might seem, you're generally not too far from help. It might have taken you 5 days to walk to where you are, but chances are that if you look at your map, you'll see a network of side trails and old roads leading back to civilization. After making the victim comfortable and treating for shock, going for help is the most effective first aid you can render.

Walking out. If you don't think you'll be able to get help within about 12 hours, walk out with the victim—it's quicker than trying a carry. Splint the injury (without, however, constricting it).

GASTROINTESTINAL ILLNESS: PREVENTION

Sanitation. Matters of personal sanitation tend to be ignored in the woods, especially after a couple of days, when you start to smell like a combination of old socks, mosquito repellent, and sweat. You can stink all you like, but take care of the basics: Wash your hands after relieving yourself and before preparing food. Keep your dishes clean. Some experts who have studied backcountry health believe that bad sanitation is just as responsible for gastrointestinal illness as bad water. And maybe more.

Water purification. Water purification is covered in chapter 8. Suffice it to say here that if you do not treat your water by boiling, filtering, or chemically purifying it, you are inviting a host of microscopic ne'er-do-wells to take up residence in your innards. Your innards are not going to be happy about this. They are going to make sure that you are not happy about this.

Watch what you drink. Even if you are treating all of your water, try to take it from the purest sources possible: the source of a spring, not the pool below it; the snowmelt dripping from a snowbank, not the stream 200 yards below. Be especially careful below tree line, in ranch country, and at water sources below areas of human activity such as campgrounds, old mining areas, and pesticide-treated fields.

GASTROINTESTINAL ILLNESS: TREATMENT

Over-the-counter drugs. Drugs like Imodium and Pepto Bismol treat symptoms, not causes; in other words, you'll feel better, but the problem is still there. Nonetheless, in the backcountry they can render a huge, albeit temporary improvement in a mighty miserable condition. Most bacterial intestinal infections usually go away if untreated—if you can put up with the discomfort for a week or more! Prescription antibiotics have an immediate effect, but don't just ingest the ones left over from some long-forgotten illness; some gastrointestinal problems require very specific drugs. For example, giardiasis is treated by a drug called Flagyl. You can pop all the antibiotic pills left over from your last case of bronchitis, but if they're not Flagyl, it's not going to do a bit of good.

Food. When recovering, avoid uncooked vegetables and fruits. Rice, bananas, oatmeal, plain crackers, and cooked carrots are good choices.

Rehydration. An extended bout of diarrhea can cause severe dehydration. To rehydrate, drink a solution of 1 quart of water containing a teaspoon of salt and a teaspoon of sugar. Try to avoid drinking water that is very cold.

HYPOTHERMIA: PREVENTION

Avoid exposure. Wind plus wet plus cold equals trouble. Check the weather forecast. Take a rest day. Use your common sense. In cold weather, think hypothermia; just as in hot-weather hiking, you think rehydration. Hypothermia kills, and if you're out in cold weather, this is something you should never, ever forget.

Recognize the symptoms. The early warning signs that you are at risk for hypothermia, including shivering and the feeling of cold, are, in fact, the human body's normal response to cold. At this stage, it may be enough to simply put on a hat or an extra layer, and take a brisk jaunt up a hill. The next stages are more severe: The victim may clench muscles and contort in an effort to keep warm. The face becomes pale; blood pressure and pulse both drop, and the victim may make errors of judgment (commonly, forgetting a mitten or losing a hat). As the body temperature further decreases, the victim slips into severe hypothermia, characterized by sluggishness, slurred speech, and poor motor coordination. Other symptoms (and evidence that the situation has become life-threatening) include some or all of the following: uncontrollable, spastic shivering; irrational, erratic behavior; sudden wild bursts of energy; the inability to focus or respond to questions; and violent reactions to suggestions or offers of help. In the final stages, the victim may suffer vision impairment and slip into unconsciousness.

Terminate exposure. If you're caught suddenly in drastically deteriorating weather conditions, and you're already fatigued and cold and wet, don't try to tough it out, even if toughing it out means just walking another mile to shelter. Look for shelter from the prevailing winds. Get out of wet clothing and put on extra layers of dry clothing, including a waterproof outer shell and a hat. Shivering is your body's way of trying to warm itself. It's also its way of saying, "Look, stupid, time to do something different." Repeat: If you are feeling dangerously cold, you are, in fact, dangerously cold and you need to do something immediately. See the next section.

HYPOTHERMIA: TREATMENT

Stop heat loss. Any hypothermia symptoms should be regarded as serious, and the immediate treatment for all stages of hypothermia is the same as prevention: Stop the heat loss. Find shelter behind a windbreak, or put up a tent; get out of wet clothes; sit or lie on a foam pad (for insulation from the cold ground); cover up with a sleeping bag; put on a hat and dry socks. In the case of mild hypothermia, these actions may be enough to terminate the hypothermic condition.

Warm drinks. This is one of the best ways to warm up someone who is borderline hypothermic. But don't fuss with stoves and hot water before stopping heat loss via shelter and dry clothing. Do not try to give hot liquids to a semi-conscious victim.

Severe hypothermia. Hypothermia turns life-threatening when the body temperature is so low that victims cannot rewarm themselves, even after heat loss is stopped. People in this condition are chilled to the bone—literally. Even more accurately, they are chilled to the heart. If victims display symptoms of severe hypothermia (especially mental impairment), the hiking partner has to take charge. As above, the first step is to stop heat loss. The next step is to try to warm the victim—but this is extremely tricky. Warning: Do not try to reverse heat loss by means of body-to-body contact. This old-fashioned method is outdated and dangerous. Blood pools in the muscles and fills with lactic acid. When the surface of the skin is warmed, this lactic-acid cocktail goes straight to the heart, where it can cause cardiac arrest. Instead, try to warm venal blood (major veins found near the armpits and groin) by means of chemical heat packs or a warm water bottle.

HYPERTHERMIA AND DEHYDRATION: PREVENTION AND TREATMENT

Dehydration is such an important issue that we've devoted an entire chapter to water: treating it, finding it, and thinking about it (see chapter 8). One of the prime causes of hyperthermia (and a whole lot of other maladies) is not drinking enough water. Guess what the most effective treatment is? Right: Drink water. In addition to water, Gatorade and bouillon broth are good; they help restore lost electrolytes.

Heat exhaustion. Symptoms include light-headedness, nausea, headache, clammy skin, and a rapid pulse. Prevention is a matter of keeping cool. Take shade breaks, stream breaks, and water breaks, and use some of the other strategies discussed in the Hot-weather Backpacking section of chapter 6, Weather. Treatment involves resting, drinking, and cooling off.

Heat stroke. Much more serious than heat exhaustion, heat stroke is characterized by a high temperature and dry—not sweaty—skin. Prevention, as always, is the best cure. Be sure not to overexert in hot weather; take shade breaks; drink water often; and don't hesitate to cut back on your mileage goals. Treatment: Reduce the body temperature immediately. Water, or clothing soaked in water, can bring down the temperature. Heat stroke can be fatal. Even if the victim has responded to treatment, always evacuate; heat stroke victims may have suffered internal damage and should be evaluated at a hospital.

ALTITUDE SICKNESS: PREVENTION

Acclimatize. People have been to the top of Mount Everest without oxygen—okay, not many of them, and at the cost of a loss of brain cells that most of us wouldn't care to contemplate. But as a backpacker, you're not headed for the top of Everest. You may, however, be headed to altitudes where you will be subject to acute mountain sickness (otherwise called altitude sickness). You may feel shortness of breath at elevations as low as 5,000 or 6,000 feet. Most hikers can easily handle elevations of 10,000, 12,000, or even 14,000 feet as long as they take time to acclimatize. Above 16,000 feet or so, some people find it difficult to adjust to the altitude. Hikers can follow a hiking trail as high as it goes with little risk of acute mountain sickness, but in order to do so, they *must* follow the most basic rule of high-altitude safety: Climb slowly. If you fly to Colorado from sea level, take a couple of ultra-low-mileage days to get used to the thinner air. Your body can adapt—if you give it enough time.

Climb high, sleep low. Choose a low-elevation campsite at the end of a day of walking at altitude. Your body gets a chance to acclimatize (during the day) and recover (at night). The next day, you'll be able to go higher more comfortably.

Check your ego at the base of the mountain. Not everyone acclimates at the same rate. A very fit person may take longer than an average Jane; the effects of altitude are persnickety and arbitrary.

Drink plenty of water. It's the most effective preventive thing you can do.

Diamox. This is a drug used by some climbers to override the body's natural responses to altitude. It's controversial in climbing circles (some people say it gives a false sense of security). Backpackers shouldn't need it; as a hiker, you're not climbing as fast or as high. However, the one exception is people whose sea-level homes are within a short drive of major mountains, like residents of the coastal region of the Pacific Northwest. If you can't resist the urge to run up something big without acclimatizing, consider using Diamox.

If in doubt, assume it's altitude sickness. Symptoms of the early onset of acute mountain sickness include headaches, slight nausea, dizziness, heart palpitations, and shortness of breath. If you have any of these symptoms, do not look around for something else to blame them on (that cold you had last month, your menstrual period, or stress at the office). You are showing signs of altitude sickness.

Severe symptoms. If not treated, symptoms can become more severe: vomiting, rapid pulse, cyanosis (bluish coloring of the skin), ragged breathing, and white or bloody sputum. Do not ignore these symptoms; the end result can be fatal pulmonary or cerebral edema.

ALTITUDE SICKNESS: TREATMENT

Breathing technique. Here's a high-mountain breathing technique that helps you control your breathing and is so effective it can actually ameliorate an altitude-induced headache. The trick is to concentrate only on exhaling. Push the air out of your lungs through pursed lips as violently as you can. Pretend you're trying to blow out a candle held at arm's length from your face. Do this each time you breathe.

Stop for a rest day. Minor symptoms might very well go away if you give yourself a chance to acclimatize. Spend a day futzing around camp. Chances are you'll feel fine the next morning.

Go downhill. If symptoms persist or intensify, go downhill to the last elevation at which you felt comfortable.

Your hiking partner. Like hypothermia, acute mountain sickness robs victims of their ability to make rational decisions. You have to stay with a hiking partner who has altitude sickness because victims can't take care of themselves.

EVACUATION AND RESCUE

Check your map. The American Red Cross teaches that the first thing you do is call for help. In the woods, that may or may not be an option. But before you assume it isn't, check your map. Using side trails or old roads, you might find that help is not as far away as you think.

Using what's on hand. Almost anything that is out of place can attract the attention of someone who is looking for you. Examples include a bright ground cloth, the reflective metal side of a space blanket, or spread-out gear (see Figure 9).

Three pumpkins means trouble. Okay, so you're not carrying a pumpkin. But the number three and the color orange are understood as symbols of trouble. Laying out three pieces of orange gear in a triangle on the ground makes you visible from the air, and it sends a clear message that you need help.

Signaling with fires. To make your fire smoky (and more visible), use wet wood or sprinkle water on it. Three fires are more visible than one, and send a message that someone's in trouble, besides. Make sure to build the fire out in the open—not under a canopy of trees!

Police whistle. This carries much farther than the human voice. Three blasts, repeated, mean trouble.

Morse code. SOS is three short, three long, three short.

Figure 9. Ground-to-air signals. Use anything that will be visible from the air; brightly colored clothing is a good choice. (a) Need food and water (b) Injured: need a doctor (c) All is well (d) Need medical supplies (e) Safe to land (f) Unable to proceed.

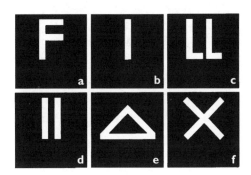

Drink untreated water and you are gambling with your health. *Always* treat backcountry water. (Photo: ©Jeff Scher)

CHAPTER 8

WATER

Finding It, Treating It, and Avoiding Parasitic Distress

THINK ABOUT DEHYDRATION, and what kinds of images pop into your mind? Blazing heat, deserts, a coyote dying of thirst under a thorn bush. And sure, when it's 110 degrees in the desert, you need copious amounts of water to get you from one campsite to the next.

But dehydration is an insidious threat in other environments, like the snowy slopes of high mountains, or on a cold-weather camping trip. You might not even notice you're becoming dehydrated in a colder climate, but dehydration can quickly exacerbate altitude sickness and hypothermia.

Consider the average hiker's body. Made up of something to the order of 70 percent water, it is continually working, climbing, and sweating its way up mountains. As it does, it loses water. Under a hot desert sun, or in dry, cold air, moisture on the skin evaporates so quickly that the hiker doesn't even feel a sensation of sweat. And then there's breathing: You lose water vapor every time you exhale, and the average hiker, whose muscles need a constant supply of oxygen, does a lot more exhaling than his cousin the couch potato. Put yourself at altitude, and the thin, dry air steals water every time you breathe.

So how much water should you drink? The answer varies tremendously, depending on altitude, humidity, exertion, temperature, and your own body's fitness and needs. Rangers at Grand Canyon National Park recommend 2 gallons per person for a full day of hot-weather desert hiking, and in my experience, that's right on the money. In cooler climes, you may be able to hike on less than 1 gallon a day. The important thing is that you pay attention: to your body, to your thirst, to your environment, to your map. A thirsty hiker is a miserable hiker. That is a promise.

But—here's the hard part—you can't just dip your canteen into a running mountain stream. The sad fact is that over the last decade or so, contamination of backcountry water has become virtually an epidemic. Pollutants and organic infestations make drinking untreated water a matter of gambling with your health. The risk: contracting a gastrointestinal illness like giardiasis in the backcountry. People who insist on learning from their own mistakes eventually learn that this is a serious one to make. If you spend a lot of time in the backcountry and don't treat your water, you will get sick. If you haven't yet, it's only a matter of time.

▲ ▲ ▲

Essential Item: Water

Why do you need it? Though humans can go several weeks without food, we can only go a few days without water. Why do you need to carry it with you? Because the spring might be dry. Because a dead antelope might be floating in the spring. Because you might get lost. Because you might not be able to make it the 5 miles to the nearest water. Because you're thirsty on a climb. Because being adequately hydrated affects everything from how happily you hike to how healthy you stay. Lack of water increases blood pressure. The blood thickens and is not as efficient at transporting nutrients to muscles. An inefficient body is more susceptible to hypothermia, hyperthermia, and altitude sickness. Without enough water, your body's muscles and organs simply can't perform as well. Completely deprived of water, they can't perform at all.

Drink before you are thirsty. Drink whether you want to or not. Make it a habit.

BOILING

Advantages and disadvantages. Boiling water is the time-tested way to kill whatever intends to ail you. It takes a lot of fuel, though, and if you use a fire, you violate a minimum-impact practice and your water tastes of woodsmoke. If you boil water over a fire, try decanting it to get rid of the ashy taste. Or throw in a couple of herbal tea bags.

How much boiling is enough? There's a lot of misinformation out there, mostly provided by overly cautious government agencies. You'll occasionally see recommendations to boil all drinking water for 5 minutes, 10 minutes, 10 minutes plus 1 minute per 1,000 feet of altitude—or even longer. If you start figuring out fuel consumption, you quickly realize that compliance creates a major feasibility problem. Take heart: Many scientists (and most backpackers) consider a rolling boil at any altitude to be sufficient for killing cooties. The Centers for Disease Control recommends 3 minutes to make sure everything—including hardier viruses—is completely dead. The Mountaineers recommends 5 minutes to be on the safe side at any altitude.

Hot water bottles. On cold nights, boil water before you go to bed. Use it as a hot water bottle before you go to sleep. You'll appreciate being able to sip from a warm bottle during the night, and in the morning, you'll have treated water to travel with during the day.

CHEMICAL TREATMENTS

Iodine. Lightweight, reliable, and trouble-free, iodine is a long-time hiker favorite. Iodine is available in liquid, crystals, or tablets. While effective against *Giardia*, it does not kill the most recent newcomer to the neighborhood of parasites, an organism called *Cryptosporidium*, which causes giardiasislike symptoms and has no cure (the disease runs its course in 7 to 10 days).

Using iodine. How effectively iodine kills cooties is a function of how much you use and how much time you give it to do its job. In cold water, it needs more time—as much as 20 minutes—or a greater dosage.

That awful taste. Potable Aqua, the maker of those incredibly teeny iodine tablets, also makes a tablet to counter the taste of iodinated water. It takes a little more time to work. A drop or two of lemon juice can also mask the flavor. Or use powdered drink mixes.

Carry iodine. Even if you prefer to filter, have iodine tablets with you. Iodine pills are hassle-free, and that can make a big difference in an emergency or bad weather. Some hikers admit they sometimes don't drink enough water because filtering is a bother. A few iodine tablets eliminate the hassle factor. Do note, however, that iodine is not safe for long-term, constant use. If you are a long-distance hiker, iodine should be your backup method, not your primary one.

FILTERS

How water filters work. Filters strain out the fugglies. The result is clean water that is a lot more aesthetically pleasing than the other two options, which effectively vanquish the armies of intestine invaders, but leave their corpses floating in your canteens.

Which filter? So-called "absolute" pore size is key. This means that nothing bigger than the listed pore size can squeeze through the filter. Most serious backcountry filters have absolute pore sizes of 1 micron or less; that'll take care of both *Giardia* and *Cryptosporidium*. Don't feel you need to buy the heaviest, most expensive filter on the market, however. Small, light filters such as the PUR Hiker can be an economical, effective alternative to bigger, weightier—and costlier— models, as long as they have a small enough absolute pore size.

Viruses. Warning: Filter pore sizes are not small enough to filter out viruses. Some filters also have an iodine element. If yours doesn't, consider taking along a vial of iodine if you're traveling in a less-developed country.

Making the job easier. Anything you can do to keep gunk away from the filter element delays clogging, which is the number-one cause of filter malfunctioning. Choose the cleanest water possible. If you must use cloudy, silt-laden water, let it sit for a while before you even try to filter it. If you're filtering directly from the source, use a float to keep your intake tube off of the river or lake bottom, and try to filter from slower-running water that doesn't contain as much churned-up, filter-clogging debris.

Filtering really gunky water. Try getting out the heavy-duty junk by pouring water through a bandanna or cheesecloth; then decant it, like you would wine, from one water bottle to another. *Then* use a prefilter to take out particles that could clog the main filter element.

A filtering device pulls water into an intake tube, passes it through a filter, and then expels it through an outtake tube. (Photo: Jeff Scher © ERG)

Once it clogs. And it will. The gunk that clogs it up is the gunk that it's removing from your water. Filters are the one piece of gear that get vilified for doing their jobs. Make sure you take your filter's directions into the field with you. Some filters can be cleaned by scrubbing the element. Others can be wiped clean. Some require replacement cartridges; if you aren't carrying one, you're out of luck.

Scrubbing. Brushing your filter's ceramic element with a retired toothbrush removes most of the gunk that causes filters to spurt, squirt, backfire, and otherwise behave like a circa 1958 automobile that's spent the last forty years in somebody's barn.

Backwashing. This is a temporary fix. Reverse the intake and output tubes, then pump backward so the water flushes the gunk out of the filter element. After backwashing, always run clean water—preferably treated with iodine or bleach—through the filter and its hoses.

Pump the unit dry. After using the filter, pump out any extra water so the water won't dribble all over its pack mates. Be especially careful in freezing temperatures; ice won't cause permanent harm, but it clogs up the works.

PREVENTING DEHYDRATION

A happy mountaineer voids clear. There's a ridiculously simple way to make sure you're drinking enough water: Check your urine. It should be clear or light yellow, not dark yellow or (worse) gold. If you're voiding clear several times a day, you're in good shape. This is especially important at altitude or in cold weather, where colder temperatures make you less aware of thirst. Exerting at altitude means that you're working and breathing harder (there's less oxygen, so respiration has to increase). Pay attention!

Think water source to water source. In an area with plenty of water, you might carry only ½ quart. In a desert, the next water source might be 2 or 3 days away. In arid climates where water is scarce, drink whenever there is a water source—whether you are thirsty or not. Even in areas with lots of water, you should have water on your mind. The worst feeling in a hiker's day might be running out of water on a big climb and then learning that there isn't any more until a few miles down the other side!

Drink before you need to. Start at the beginning of the day, and at every chance thereafter. A quart before you start walking, and a quart before you start a climb, makes a big difference in how you feel and perform.

Keep water at arm's reach. Once you hike with one of those water bottle–carrying systems that put your water at arm's reach at all times, you'll be hooked. Keeping your water where you can easily get your hands on it—that is, without having to take off your pack every time you want to take a drink—means that you will drink more often. Many packs now come with pouches or attachments that put water at your fingertips.

Treating dehydration. Two common causes of dehydration are heat and intestinal problems. A solution of 1 quart of water with one teaspoon each of salt and sugar can help replenish fluids.

CARRYING WATER

Fabric water bags. Fabric water carriers hold from 2 to 8 quarts and enable you to carry water from stream to camp without making repeated trips. When empty, they take up next to no space in your pack. You can also use them to carry water for a dry camp if you're hiking in arid terrain where water sources are many miles apart. Choose the toughest, most rugged water carrier you can find, along with some way to repair it should it get snagged by a cactus needle. Duct tape will do.

Carrying large loads. If you have to carry a lot of water, remember what they say about putting all of your eggs in one basket. Several small containers are better than one big one; if a container leaks, you won't lose all your water. If you carry water in fabric bags, be sure you trust the spout to stay shut. If in doubt, carry the water bag outside your pack, where you'll feel any dripping before you lose your water and soak your gear. This is something to experiment with before you're out in the desert with a leaky valve.

Packing a bulky water load. Water is not only heavy, it takes up space. If you have to take on extra water, be extra certain that you've pared down your load as much as possible . (Fortunately, in the kinds of conditions where water is scarce—like a desert—you usually don't need quite as much gear.) You might have to strap some of your gear, or your water bags, to the outside of your pack. Use straps or elastic cords to secure them in place so your load doesn't slosh around as you walk.

Emergency water bags. In a pinch, use a sturdy resealable plastic bag reinforced with duct tape to carry water. This is only a short-term solution!!! If you're on a long hike and your water bag goes bust, don't despair. In a small town, buy a gallon "box" of wine. The plastic bladder and valve inside the box are almost exactly the same as those used in many fabric-covered water bags. Of course, you can also tie a 1-gallon plastic jug to the back of your pack to use for carrying water short distances from stream to camp.

Wide-mouth bottles. Always choose wide-mouth water bottles. They are easier to fill in shallow pools, and if the pool is so shallow that even that doesn't work, you can use the lid to spoon water into your containers. In winter, wide-mouthed bottles are easier to fill with snow. They are easier to put drink mixes into, easier to remove chunks of ice from, and easier to clean.

FINDING WATER

Talk to locals. Find out if it's been a dry year or a wet year. Ask about the springs on your route; knowledgeable locals can tell you if they are reliable or constantly dry. Make sure you and the person you are talking to are using the same vocabulary. Some people (even those who work for land management agencies) might assume you are asking about potable water from a faucet. So ask about stock tanks, springs, and windmills, and specify that you'll be treating the water yourself.

Look for the green. In arid terrain, any speck of water supports an ecosystem of plants and animals. Cottonwoods are an excellent indication that there is water nearby, and if you're heading for a place called Cottonwood Spring, you'll almost always hit pay dirt. (Do not, however, make a habit of trusting nomenclature. One of the driest places I know is a place on the Pacific Crest Trail called Whitewater Canyon.) Willows—especially dense, continuous thickets—are also a good indication, although not quite as reliable as cottonwoods because willows can grow along seasonal water sources as well as permanent

In dry terrain, willows are a fairly reliable sign of water. (Photo: ©Karen Berger/Daniel R. Smith)

Look for clusters of trees, especially aspen, in a drainage gully, and you might find water by digging down a few inches. (Photo: ©Karen Berger/ Daniel R. Smith)

ones. In alpine areas, following a thicket of willows downstream eventually yields water and, sometimes, digging a hole in a willow thicket will yield water. In very dry terrain, aspen trees can be a water indicator. (Aspens need 15 inches of rainfall annually to grow. If you see them in a region that has less rainfall than that, they may be tapping into an underground source, a drainage, or a spring).

Notice seasonal patterns. Patterns tend to repeat themselves. If you pass several seasonal streams (marked in dotted or light blue on most maps) that are dry, chances are that you're hiking during a season in which most, if not all, seasonal sources are dry. Don't make the mistake of thinking that if you just push on to the next one, the pattern will reverse itself. Instead, start thinking about alternate sources like springs, windmills, or permanent water courses.

Go downstream. Just because a water source is dry in one place doesn't mean it's dry through its entire course. During the dry season or after a drought, water in seasonal streams frequently goes underground and reappears somewhere else.

Look under a rock. In a streambed, the shady areas under rocks sometimes collect pools of water that evaporate more slowly because they're not in direct sun.

Look for animal tracks. Animals need to drink, too, and animal paths often lead to water. Look for concentrations of scat and tracks. Domesticated animals like cattle and horses require reliable water sources; if you see a huge herd of them, they're likely to be near water.

Look for old buildings. It's only logical; the people who built those old cabins needed a nearby source of water. But don't depend on wells marked on your out-of-date USGS map; wells can be defunct, broken, or sealed shut.

Even in inhospitable places like Wyoming's Great Divide Basin, there is usually some water somewhere. Look for ruined old houses—settlers tended to build near reliable sources. (Photo: ©Karen Berger/Daniel R. Smith)

MARGINAL WATER SOURCES

Make a funnel. If your water source is a mere dribbling trickle, use a broad leaf to make a funnel. Two other things to try: the tent sleeve tube from your emergency kit, and the windscreen from your stove.

Out-of-reach sources. If water is available but down and out of your reach, you can get at it if you have a water bottle with the lid attached to the body. Tie a length of cord to the plastic doohickey that affixes the lid to the water bottle. Weight the bottle with stones, then lower it into an otherwise inaccessible water source (see Figure 10). If your cook pot has a wire handle, you can do the same thing with it.

Figure 10. To get to hard-to-reach water, put some stones in a water bottle, and tie a length of parachute cord to the strap that holds the lid. The weight of the stones will make the bottle sink.

Sudden thunderstorms. A tarp, ground cloth, or rain fly can be used to collect water from a sudden storm.

Make an evaporation still. This is an emergency strategy only. Real life presents a whole host of obstacles: just for one, how do you dig a hole in hard, compacted desert soil if (presumably) you're not carrying a spade or a shovel? Nonetheless, for what it's worth (and in a real emergency, it could be worth plenty), see Figure 11 to learn how to make a solar still.

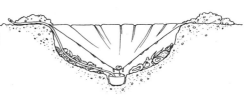

Figure 11. Construct a solar evaporation still using a tarp, a stone, a length of tube, a water bottle, and whatever vegetation happens to be nearby.

COLD-WEATHER WATER

Treating winter water. Should you or shouldn't you? Just because it's cold doesn't mean you're safe: *Giardia* thrives in cold running water. Treat all surface water, just as you would during the warmer seasons. As far as snowmelt is concerned, use your judgment. There could be elk or other animal scat in the immediate vicinity. Be sure to treat any water coming from a discolored snowbank. The red blush you sometimes see on alpine snow is actually an alga that can make you sick.

Finding running water. Take advantage of any sources of running water, because it takes a lot of fuel to melt snow. Larger bodies of water, especially fast-running water, freeze more slowly. If you're carrying an ice ax, you can sometimes chop a hole in the ice, especially if it isn't very thick. Careful that you don't fall in! And remember—running water needs to be treated.

Melting snow for water. Think "burning water" is just an expression? You'll find out otherwise if you try to melt snow by throwing a heap of it into your cook pot. The snow goes directly from solid to gas, and scorches on the bottom of the pan. Instead, start with an inch or so of water, and then add snow slowly.

Mining snow. It takes a lot of snow to make a pot of water (the amount varies according to how powdery the snow is: Dense, wet "Cascade concrete" yields more water than a similar volume of fluffy dry Colorado snow). Collect snow in a big black garbage bag. (Hint: Use a small shovel, which is an essential piece of gear for winter trips.) This way, you'll have a big pile of clean snow all in one place, and the black bag will absorb the sun's rays and warm the snow so it doesn't take as much time (and fuel) to melt in your pot.

Warming water. Many hikers don't drink enough water in cold weather because barely melted snow is just too cold to drink. Once you have a couple of bottles of water, put them under a dark stuff sack or garbage bag and let them warm in the sun. Or go ahead and use a little extra fuel to warm the water so it's comfortable to drink.

Hot springs. Never drink directly from a hot spring. Hot springs support ecosystems of heat-tolerating organisms, some of which are toxic to humans. Bathing in hot springs is usually fine (but avoid putting your head underwater unless you've been told it's safe by a ranger; in rare cases, hot springs harbor organisms that can attack human respiratory tissues). You can, however, use the heat from hot springs to melt snow. Just immerse your snow-filled bottles in the spring, wait till the snow melts, then add more and do it again.

Winter water bottles. For cold-weather camping, choose water bottles with heavy-duty lids that have several tiers of threading. In winter, you put both hot and cold drinks in your water bottles; the heavy-duty threading is more likely to withstand temperature changes. Newer, fancier water bottles with protective caps (to keep out the dirt) have hinges and parts that tend to freeze in really cold weather. Stick with the simple stuff.

Boiling water and plastic bottles. If you pour boiling water directly into your water bottles, be sure to leave the lids on loosely as they cool. Open the lids every half hour or so to let some steam escape. If you forget, your plastic water bottles will collapse and contort into weird shapes as the liquid cools and loses volume.

Sleeping with water bottles. In just-around-the-freezing-point weather, it's okay to leave your water bottles in the tent vestibule. Put them upside down so that any ice that forms does so at the bottom of the bottle (that is, away from the lid). In really cold weather, take water bottles inside the tent with you—or even in your sleeping bag. Make sure you've tested the water bottles and found them leakproof.

Leaving water out. You can also bury a water bottle in the snow. Snow is a good insulator, and the temperature inside a snowbank is, curiously, not cold enough to freeze your water. Mark the place with a ski pole or ice ax; you want to be able to find that water in the morning. Don't forget your water bag; empty it, bury it in snow, or bring it inside. A water bag filled with a block of ice is a heavy, useless nuisance.

Frozen water bottle lids. Turn the bottle upside down and immerse it for a moment in a pot of warm water. If you don't have your stove on, loosen the lid by putting the bottle under your jacket and letting it warm up for a minute or two. Do this while you're still warm and cozy in your sleeping bag, or just before you start hiking. Standing around in the cold with an icy bottle next to your chest can only lead to discomfort.

Insulators. Commercial fabric insulators for water bottles are available. They're lighweight, squashable (i.e., packable), and effective. But you can make your own with an old piece of foam pad. Cut out a rectangle (one side the same length as the height of the water bottle, and one side the same length as the circumference of the water bottle) and wrap it loosely around your bottle. Then cut out a circle roughly the size of your water bottle's bottom, and use duct tape to tape it to the bottom of the tube. Think of those drink insulators people take to ball games—that's the idea.

CHAPTER 9

FIELD REPAIRS

—

Beyond Safety Pins and Duct Tape

SOONER OR LATER, something is going to break or snap or rip or—in the case of your stove—fall into a state of stubborn, implacable silence. When it does (and you can just about guarantee that it won't happen on a perfect sunny day), you have to fix it, jury-rig an alternative, live without it—or pack up and go home. A trip-ending breakdown doesn't have to involve some complex component of a high-tech piece of equipment. Small, simple things can derail an adventure just as completely as big complicated things. Like if someone steps on your pack's waistbelt buckle and it cracks in two.

You can't prepare for everything that could possibly go wrong. You can't carry two stoves in case one breaks, or two tents in case a pole snaps and rips the rain fly. What you can do, however, is pretty powerful. You can know your gear and how it works. You can choose gear that is simple and functional and does what it's supposed to do without a whole lot of unnecessary extras. (It's better to select a simple, pared-down version of a high-quality item than to buy a bells-and-whistles extravaganza made by a less rigorous manufacturer.) You can take care of it properly by reading the instructions and following all those detailed, picky little directions. And you can carry a repair kit that gives you the tools to figure out some kind of workable solution for all but the most improbable and disastrous predicaments.

In my 10,000-plus miles of backpacking, I've had a few unfixable problems (like the walking sticks that snapped in half, the boots that delaminated so that the soles slapped like peeling banana skins, or the water filter that said "no way, no how" to the prospect of cleaning sludge that I was trying to pretend was water one dry, hot day in New Mexico). But I've never had to end a trip, and I've only once gone to sleep without a hot meal. Good gear is made to last, and it generally does. Knowing how to use it and take care of it prolongs its life. And a decent repair kit, along with a bit of ingenuity, can generally get you to the next road crossing or even, quite happily, to the end of your trip.

THE REPAIR KIT

There's no such thing as the perfect repair kit, a lesson I learn on each new trip when I make small adjustments in what I take. Sometimes I miss what I left behind. Usually, however, I've got some combination of most of the following.

Needles. Bring several different-sized needles, including a thick needle with a big hole (like a carpet needle) that can punch through pack cloth. We're not talking delicate needlework: Your heavy-duty needles should be able to thread a strand of dental floss. Store needles in a film canister (along with buttons, pins, and other losables), or stick them into a matchbook.

Thread. Bring several weights of thread: heavy-duty thread (like carpet thread), dental floss, and standard thread. Don't use heavy-duty thread for normal repairs on regular clothing because the tension of extra-strong thread actually causes the fabric to tear more.

Wire. A couple of yards of thin wire can help hold things together.

Thimble. You need it to force a needle through tough fabric like several layers of cordura pack cloth. Try one of those teeny little plastic jobs that come with hotel sewing kits. For real sewing, it's virtually useless. But it weighs nothing, it's bright orange so it's hard to lose, and, for a couple of stitches on the trail, it does the job. For truly stubborn fabrics, you may be better off using the lock-stitcher found on most Swiss Army knives.

Safety pins. Lots of different sizes are a good idea, especially big, heavy-duty diaper pins with latches that lock them shut.

Tape. Bring two kinds: duct tape and white medicine tape (to be used interchangeably, or whichever works best). Wrap several yards of duct tape around a spare pen. That way, you won't be tempted to use (read: lose) the spare pen, which can be vital for communicating in an emergency. You can also wrap duct tape around a fuel bottle; a few layers of tape adds a little insulation between the super-cold fuel and your fingers, and could save your fingers from frostbite.

Velcro. Tape-on strips can hold together sleeping bags and rain gear that have suffered a zipper disaster.

Small pliers. Use these for repairing zippers and air-mattress valves.

Cord. Regular parachute cord is a good multiuse tool. In addition to bear bagging and laundry-line duty, you can use it to lash things onto your pack, tie broken parts together, guy line a tent, or hold up a tarp.

Glue. Urethane-based glues like Shoe Goo or Free-sole are the hiker's choice for boot repairs. But most hikers don't prepare surfaces properly (i.e., clean them thoroughly), clamp their repairs together, and wait out the holding time, so field repairs of boot soles rarely hold for long. Still, they're better than nothing, and usually keep you going until you can get to a cobbler. These glues are also useful for affixing repair patches to your air mattress and your clothing.

Spare stove parts. These are generally useless unless you bring along the instructions that came with your stove. A spare parts kit generally contains a multipurpose stove tool, a jet cleaning tool (if necessary), a spare pump cup and O-rings, pump oil, and extra parts like replacement jets or adapters for different kinds of fuel.

Pocket knife. Your pocket knife is one of the Ten Essentials. But you can expand on the plain two-bladed pocket knife by using a Swiss Army–type knife. Most hikers choose one that has a couple of cutting blades, a bottle opener, a can opener, scissors, tweezers, a hole punch, and maybe a corkscrew.

Tweezers. Throw in a spare pair of good ones in case the little miniature tweezers on your pocket knife get lost. They're especially critical in desert hiking.

Film canisters. These are useful for storing easy-to-lose items.

Zipper parts. Bring heads and sliders to fit your important gear: rain jacket and pants, tent, and sleeping bag. To make effective zipper repairs, you'll need a small pair of pliers, too.

Self-adhesive patches and ripstop repair tape. Bring several feet of it, for patching up ripped rain gear and tents. Warning: You shouldn't dry-clean your outdoor gear anyway, but especially don't dry-clean anything with repair tape on it if you want the repair to outlast the cleaning process.

Spare stuff. Bring such things as cord locks, buckles, buttons (various sizes), rawhide shoelaces, batteries, a flashlight bulb (check to see if your headlamp already has one hidden in the housing somewhere; if not, pack a spare in cotton swabs and store it in a film canister).

Clevis pins. These are used for holding straps to external-frame packs. You can also use them as zipper pulls.

Alcohol swabs. Use these for cleaning gear before you attempt to repair it with adhesives. These are also a first-aid item for disinfecting wounds, blisters, or needles that you intend to use to pierce a blister.

Hose clamps. These are useful for busted external-frame packs. Hose clamps also come in handy for splinting tent poles. And if you're traveling on skis, you can use them for broken skis and poles.

▲ ▲ ▲

Used Gear

Good backpacking gear is made to last. It's well-designed and attractive—and fashionable. So fashionable that much of the outdoor clothing that's bought today isn't even used for outdoor sports—it's worn in city high schools and suburban shopping malls. And many of the tents and sleeping bags and packs sold today spend much of their lives in attics or closets, go outdoors a handful of times, and then get discarded in favor of something newer. In other cases, people get excited about backpacking—but then find that they don't enjoy it as much as they thought they would. Or they go on to other interests.

What does this mean to you, the outdoorsperson? You can complain about our overconsumptive hyper-trendy society—or you can take advantage of it. Once you've learned how to maintain and repair your own equipment, you might find that you can gear up with perfectly good pre-owned equipment at a fraction of the price.

- Check out the back of local hiking club magazines: *The Appalachian Trail News, AMC Outdoors,* and countless smaller organizations accept classified ads for their publications. Or place an ad yourself advertising what you want to buy.
- Check your local outfitting store: Many of them have bulletin boards where they allow customers to post news of used equipment for sale.
- One reason to stay local: It's best to actually see a piece of gear before you buy it, so you can verify the condition for yourself.
- Don't get overly excited at the low prices. Be just as careful buying discounted items as you are in a store. Check quality, condition, and, most of all, fit. A great deal on nearly new boots isn't a great deal if they don't fit.
- You're buying at discount, so go for the name brands. Their guarantees say that their gear is designed to last a lifetime. The guarantee probably won't be valid because you're not the original purchaser. But high-quality manufacturers mean what they say: They make their gear to last. They also provide great customer service at a reasonable price.

PATCHING AND TAPING

Clean surfaces first. Tape adheres better to clean surfaces. Admittedly, clean surfaces are hard to come by in the backcountry, but try your best. Brush away any loose dirt, wipe clean with a damp cloth, and finish off the job with a little rubbing alcohol or white gas. Let the gear dry thoroughly before attempting to tape.

Round edges. Have you ever wondered why the patches you buy commercially come in the shape of a circle? It's because rounded edges don't catch on things, so they tend to stay on longer.

Sizing the patch. Make the patch about ½ inch larger all the way around than the area to be patched.

A smooth finish. Using a flat surface as a work surface (try a book, or turn your cook pot upside down), rub the patch smooth with the rounded edge of your pocket knife or spoon. Putting a piece of paper (if you used a commercial adhesive patch, try the backing that you pulled off of it) between your tool and the patch means you won't push up the edges by mistake.

Use glue. Adhesive patches will stay on, assuming that they're not in an area of high and constant stress. But a dab of glue doubles their life, or more.

Stitch it up. To stop a tear from growing, stitch the end of it. This is particularly effective for those corner-shaped tears you get when your clothing catches on brambles or thorns. You can also make a temporary patch permanent by stitching it on.

Prevention. Patch over a worn area before it tears. This is one of those stitch-in-time situations.

Big rips. A roll of 1- or 2-inch-wide athletic tape doubles as both a first-aid item and gear-repair tape. Tape has reliable holding power: In fact, it can adhere so strongly that it's almost impossible to remove, and if you do manage to get it off, it can leave a sticky residue that makes permanent repair impossible. Then again, if the tape insists on fixing the problem for good, why not let it?

ZIPPERS

Sliders. Many zippers are self-repairing. You pass the slider over the problem area (using gentle force, if necessary) and the slider repairs the problem. When the zipper keeps coming undone on a regular basis, try tightening the slider with a pair of pliers.

Get rid of obstacles. Check teeth for recurring problems, like caught material or globs of dirt. In the field, wipe the zipper with a bandanna. At home, spray a little silicone along the teeth.

PACKS

Plastic buckles. The plastic buckles that hold your waist belt shut are vulnerable to being stepped on whenever you leave your pack on the ground. If they split in two, you can hold them together (more or less permanently) by cutting or tearing athletic tape into ultra-thin strips

Those plastic buckles on your pack's waistband are vulnerable to being stepped on. It's best to carry a spare, but sometimes you can hold them together with tape. (Photo: ©Jeff Scher)

(no more than ¼ inch wide) and then tightly wrapping the tape several times around the buckle.

Busted pack seams. Good quality packs rarely split and tear. If yours does, a sturdy piece of wire might be your best tool for a temporary fix.

BOOT REPAIR

Delaminating boot soles. These can be held to your boots with urethane glues, but for reasons discussed in the Glue item of the Repair Kit section earlier in this chapter, most field repairs don't last

Trusty duct tape can hold almost anything together, at least for a while. Here it salvages boots that surrendered to the Pennsylvania rocks on the Appalachian Trail and delaminated 50 miles from the next town stop. (Photo: ©Karen Berger/Daniel R. Smith)

nearly as long as you'd like. Trusty duct tape is another less-than-perfect option for an emergency, assuming you have enough tape on hand. Wrap the sole to the boot with multiple layers of tape, and it'll hold for maybe 15 miles (less in wet weather) before you need to remove all the old tape and reapply new. It's an imperfect solution, but it can keep you walking.

Wire it shut. A thick piece of braided wire can help keep delaminating soles in place. Glue the soles in place, then wrap the wire around the soles and hold it in place over the toe by running it through boot-lace eyelets.

Wet boots. Do not put wet boots next to a fire. The heat all but destroys the leather. (I once saw someone walking out of the backcountry on closed-cell foam pads strapped to his feet with parachute cord—in the snow—because he had burned his boots to an unusable crisp.) Instead, let the boots dry in their own time and treat them with a little tube of leather conditioner.

MATTRESS REPAIR

Prevention. An air mattress strapped outside your pack (especially at the bottom, where you drop it and sit on it all day) is an accident waiting to happen. Double that if you're off trail, getting whacked and pricked by who-knows-what. Pack more sensibly by putting your mattress inside your pack. Or, if you insist on keeping your air mattress in harm's way, protect it with a heavy-duty stuff sack.

Mark the hole. Most air mattress problems are caused by tiny punctures. If possible, note and mark the hole with a pen. (For instance, if you actually see the cactus quill go in, mark the spot before you pull it out.)

Finding the problem. If you don't know where the hole is, inflate the mattress. Fold it in half and wet the mattress with water or (better) soapy water. Little escaping bubbles will show you where the hole is. Caution: This is more tedious than it sounds, especially with a full-sized mattress. If you are near a quiet body of water, simply immerse the entire inflated mattress and look for the escaping bubbles.

Plugging the leak. First clean the damaged area around the hole with a mild detergent and let it dry. Then deflate the mattress. Rub a drop of adhesive (urethane glue—in the repair kit) in the hole.

Larger tears. Follow the directions on your mattress's repair kit. Usually, this means deflating the mattress, cleaning the area around the tear, applying a patch (held on by glue), and putting a pot full of just-boiled water on top to hold the patch in place and let it cure.

Duct tape. It'll work in the field as a temporary patch, but you'll have a devil of a time getting the residue off at home. Better to take the repair kit along.

Burns. These are usually not reparable.

TENT REPAIR

Rips. Adhesive repair tape handles most snags and small tears, provided that the area isn't one that receives direct stress.

If you sew. Use the smallest needle possible and remember to seam-seal any sewing repairs; those little needle holes are miniature water spouts.

Leaks. Leaks are generally a function of operator error, not equipment failure. Be sure the tent is staked out tightly and that your ground

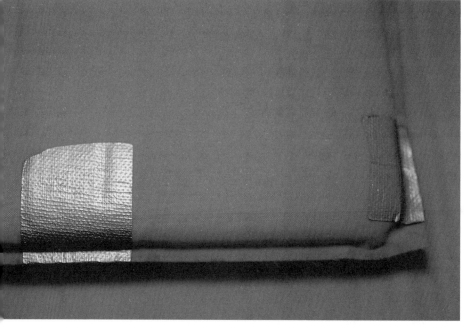

Sometimes a temporary repair can become permanent: the duct tape patch on this mattress has lasted for years. (Photo: ©Dorcas Miller)

cloth isn't sticking out from under the tent. If the tent is leaking because you didn't bother to seam-seal it, now you know why you should have done so. Unfortunately, the only thing you can do at this juncture is repeat one thousand times through the soggy night, "I *will* seam-seal my tent, I *will* seam-seal my tent. . . ."

Condensation. Water in the tent can be the result of condensation, not just a leak; ventilating the tent can prevent or ameliorate this problem.

Snapped poles. These are a cinch to splint if you packed along the aluminum pole splint the manufacturer should have included in the package when you bought the tent. Straighten out the tent poles, insert them into the splint, and hold them in place with duct tape. If you don't have the pole splint, improvise one by cutting a piece of metal from a soda can, or by using a half-moon tent stake. The half-moon stake may not work for tents with sleeves—the protruding part of the stake can rip the tent fabric. But it's a good solution for tents that use clips. If you use the soda-can fix, be sure to tape all sharp and ragged metal edges to avoid tearing the tent. See Figure 12. Note: Save yourself the hassles and buy generic pole splints at an outfitting store.

Prevention. Tent poles are particularly vulnerable to damage at the joints. Don't unfold shock-corded tent poles by throwing them up in the air and letting them wildly click into full length. Instead, put them together (and take them apart) one section at a time. This saves wear and tear on the poles, and helps avoid little raggedy burrs that can rip tent fabric. If you notice burrs, sand them smooth with rocks.

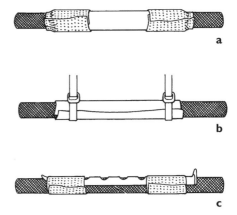

Figure 12. Fixing a cracked tent pole. (a) With a pole sleeve and duct tape (b) With metal from a soda can and a hose clamp (c) With a half-moon tent stake and duct tape.

CHAPTER 10

BETWEEN TRIPS

A Little Maintenance Prevents a Lot of Mildew

YOU'VE JUST RETURNED from a weeklong backpacking trip. Your clothes smell like the local garbage dump, your dishes are lined with a sticky residue of burnt macaroni and cheese and charbroiled oatmeal, and you've got two things on your mind: a shower and a pizza.

Be honest, now. What do you do? Jump in the shower and call for the pizza, right? Maybe you remember to stick your clothes in the laundry and put your dirty dishes in the dishwasher. Your gear probably gets thrown into the attic while you promise yourself you'll sort it out sooner—or later.

Several backpacking trips later, you wonder why your high-tech gear isn't performing up to par. You notice a couple of mold spots on your tent floor. Your sleeping bag doesn't seem to be keeping you as warm at night. The truth is, most gear isn't defeated by monsoons or Himalayan expeditions—it's defeated by neglect.

CLOTHING

Wash everything. Except for your rain gear, every item of clothing, whether it was used or not, should be washed. Even if you didn't wear it, wash it. Your wool shirt could be harboring moths picked up from that backcountry cabin.

Fabrics are fussy. Follow care directions. For instance, polypropylene is allergic to heat. Washed in hot water, it shrinks; put in a dryer, it melts. Another example: Strong detergents strip oils from wool, and the presence of oils is one of the characteristics that makes wool warm and water-resistant. Use a mild soap, clean in cold or cool water, and never put wool in the dryer. Instead, roll items in a towel to remove water and lay flat to dry.

Gore-Tex care. Wash your rain gear only when it's really starting to get foul; otherwise, turn it inside out and hang it out to air. Avoid dry-cleaning. Wash Gore-Tex in cold water with a mild powdered detergent or a product specifically designed for Gore-Tex fabrics. And don't use bleach or fabric softeners.

Leaky Gore-Tex? Maybe not. Gore-Tex feels wet when it loses its ability to shed water. Drying Gore-Tex in a dryer can help restore the shedding function; if it doesn't, try one of the durable water-repellent sprays available at your outfitters. Ironing returns water repellency and "beading" to old rain-battered Gore-Tex.

Storage. Big translucent plastic bins like you'd buy at an office supply store for holding files make good containers for hiking clothes, including all those gaiters, mittens, down booties, and hats that end up as a tangled jumble in a box somewhere.

Store wools in mothballs. You know why.

TENTS

Hose down the house. After a wet, muddy hike, put up your tent and hose it down, if necessary using a mild soap to rinse away stuck-on grime. Leave the tent up to dry.

Check the seam-sealing. Seams are your tent's Achilles' heel. The teeny little holes a needle makes when it's stitching two pieces of fabric together can let in millions of molecules of water—so much that an otherwise well-designed, perfectly good tent becomes a virtual sieve. That's why you need to seam-seal a brand-new tent. If you've already seam-sealed the tent, check to be sure the compound isn't flaking off. If it is, you may need to reapply it.

Seam-sealing. Seam-seal outside on a sunny day, so you don't breathe in fumes from the seam-sealing compound and so the compound dries quickly. Put the rain fly on upside down and seal the inside. Rub in the seam-sealing compound, let dry, and do a second coat. If you're really neurotic (read: if you really want to stay dry), seal both sides of the rain fly. Then seal any seams around the tent floor. (You don't need to seal other seams on the tent itself, because the tent body is breathable, not waterproof.) Let the seams dry. Then sprinkle on a little cornstarch, talcum powder, or sawdust before storing the tent. It eliminates the possibility of the new seam-seal sticking.

Spray-on waterproofers. Spray-on, durable waterproof coatings can help a tired old tent live a longer, drier life. But check first with the manufacturer of your tent (you'll find phone numbers for equipment manufacturers in *BACKPACKER* magazine's annual gear review). Warning: Don't use spray-ons for single-walled tents; the spray will interfere with the tent's breathability.

BOOTS

Clean your boots. Brush off dirt with a stiff wire brush. Condition the boots with a leather treatment like Biwell. Check with the manufacturer; some recommend specific products.

Sprinkle some baking soda inside. Face it, it stinks in there. A little baking soda can freshen things up.

Seam-seal. Liquid rubber or a compound like Free-sole Urethane Shoe Repair can be used to keep seams tough and waterproof.

Trouble spots. Check soles and seams, two trouble spots for heavily used boots. Boot soles that show signs of delaminating can be held together with some heavy-duty urethane-based glue, but if it's going to be a while before your next hike, you'll be far better off sending the boot out to the manufacturer or to a shop that specializes in hiking boot repair.

Supergaiter alert. Supergaiters are those boot-shaped gaiters that go over the entire boot from heel to toe, as well as up your calves. You can't beat them for adding a few degrees of warmth to cold toes. But they extract a price: They're fiendishly difficult to put on properly because the rubber bands that go around the boots are so tight. Old hands at winter camping put on a couple of dabs of glue to keep the supergaiters in place, but don't be tempted to leave them in place during the off season. The torque the supergaiters exert on the boot sole will ruin your boots.

Shoe trees. These help maintain the shape of boots that spend months on end in an attic.

SLEEPING BAGS

Down and dirty. Down sleeping bags should be washed as infrequently as possible to keep up their loft. Washing strips down of its natural oils, which, much like those of wool, waterproofs the down. Unzip your bag and air it out on a windy, sunny day. Wipe off any obvious dirt. Hint: Sleeping in your clothes, or in a lightweight silk or nylon sleeping bag liner, helps keep your bag clean longer.

Washing down. When you do wash a down sleeping bag, avoid dry-cleaning and agitator-type washing machines (the kind you have at home). Instead, choose front-loading drum-type washers. Use mild detergent, cool water, and the gentlest cycle available.

Drying down. To dry a down sleeping bag, use low heat or, better yet (if you have several hours to spare), the air-dry cycle. The "classic" method of throwing in a clean tennis shoe to separate the clumps of wet down does work, but is hard on the down and can shorten your sleeping bag's life expectancy. Instead, try using a tennis ball or a lightweight canvas shoe, and only throw it in for the last minute or two of the drying cycle.

Caution: Handling a wet bag. If you don't have hours to spend watching your sleeping bag go around and around on the low-heat or no-heat cycle, hang it up to dry, but handle it gently. The weight of the wet down can tear the baffles. (Baffles are the channels that ensure that the down inside the bag stays evenly spread over you when you're sleeping. Without baffles, the down would simply flow like liquid to one spot in the bag.) Gather the wet bag up gently. You can transport it home wrapped in an old sheet. Then hang it to dry on several parallel clotheslines that support all of its weight evenly. Even better, if you have one: Lay it on a hammock.

Storing sleeping bags. Down sleeping bags should never be stored in their stuff sacks. You'll compress their insulation and ruin their loft, and the loft is what keeps you warm. If you've got room, lay them out flat for storage. If not, put them in a cotton pillowcase. Some higher-end bags come with their own pillowcase-sized cotton storage sacks.

SLEEPING PADS

Blow before you go. Check the pad before you go on your next trip. Give it a couple of breaths to fully inflate it, and then leave it inflated overnight.

Repairing broken valves. If you don't carry pliers into the woods, this is a home repair. Repair a broken valve by simply pulling it out gently with a pair of pliers. A new one can be pushed into place and sealed there with glue.

BACKPACKS

Cleaning. A mildly dirty pack can be brushed off with a vegetable scrubber. For more serious abuse, dump the pack in a shower and clean it with a mild detergent. Make sure you check all pockets first, and shake out the pack; you'll be surprised at how much dirt will come out.

Waterproofing. After its bath, improve the water repellency of your pack by spraying on a waterproofing treatment.

Silicone spray. Sometimes packs develop irritating squeaks. Use silicone spray on squeaky pack joints.

Storage. Sure, packs are tough. But avoid careless damage: bending the stays or having the plastic buckles get stepped on. Hang the pack on a door knob, on a coat hanger in your closet, or on a bathroom hook (the plastic hooks used for hanging bathrobes) that you install in the attic.

Troubleshooting. Most pack problems involve seams that split under the stress of too much weight. Check seams periodically for signs of wearing or splitting, especially seams around the waist belt and the shoulder straps. These should be repaired professionally.

STOVES

Storing fuel. Fuel that sits around for a long time can develop minor impurities that hinder stove performance. Pour unused fuel back into its original container. The next time you go out, pour it through a fuel filter to remove any fugglies.

Clean according to manufacturer's directions. This achieves two goals: It gets your stove ready for the next trip, and it gives you a chance to familiarize yourself with a stove's innards. It's a much more pleasant way to learn than messing with a sputtering stove in the dark on a rainy night.

Oil the pump cup. If your stove has a leather pump cup, keep it supple by oiling it regularly. A small amount of mineral oil is best, but in a pinch vegetable oil will do. This is the place to look if the pump on your stove doesn't seem to be creating any pressure.

O-rings. Check the condition of your stove's O-rings before heading out for a long trip.

WATER FILTERS

Clean the filter! Scrub or wipe the filter element, per the directions, and run a quart of clean water through to see how well the filter is working. Better to find out it's time to change the filter element before the middle of your next trip!

Backwash a sluggish filter. Switch the intake and output hoses and flush out the filter.

Disinfect. After cleaning and backwashing, run a solution of 1 quart of water with a tablespoon of chlorine bleach through to disinfect the filter.

GENERAL STORAGE

Keep a gear list. Divide it into categories: sleeping (tent, sleeping bag, sleeping pad) and cooking (pots and pans, stove). That way, you cover all the bases and you can make modifications in each category without forgetting the basics.

Organizing the small stuff. Hanging multipocket shoe organizers brings order to all those first-aid supplies, filter parts, stove gizmos, and repair kit supplies.

Little things. I find that it takes me about 10 minutes to pack my big essentials (tent, stove, clothes) and hours to track down all those necessary little things: the bug dope, candle lantern, and what did I do with the Swiss Army knife? Keep a packed "ditty bag" on hand so you don't have to go hunting for the irritating, small, losable items that most of us forget about until the last minute.

For procrastinators. Do leave batteries till the last minute. You want to go out with a fresh supply. Buy the new ones that come with little gauges that show how much juice they've got left.

Stuff, don't fold. Think of the blue jeans you keep folded on a shelf in your closet. That's right: the ones with the white lines running down the legs from being folded in the same place over and over. The same goes for gear, especially tents and rain gear; if you stuff the gear

Stuff sacks are called that for a reason. If you fold gear, it will develop wear lines, which ruins the coating. (Photo: Jeff Scher © ERG)

instead, the creases will always be somewhere different, and the gear won't develop weak points in the fabric and the coating.

Zippers. You can degunk dirty zippers with the aid of a vegetable-cleaning brush. Wax with paraffin or silicone to make the mechanism work more smoothly.

Pull cords and guy lines. Add pull cords to zippers so you can easily grab them in cold weather with bulky gloves on. Hold the ends to a lighted match for a few seconds; the burnt ends won't unravel. Do the same thing for guy lines.

Cord locks. Add them to pants with drawstrings so you don't have to figure out how to thread a drawstring through a waistband some wet day when your fingers are frozen.

Water bottles. Rinse with a baking soda–water solution, then store them with their caps off. If you leave the caps on, plastic water bottles develop a nasty smell.

Go window shopping. Between trips, spend some time at your local outfitters. Technology is changing every day, and some of it is going to come up with the absolutely perfect solution to some backcountry dilemma.

PROFESSIONAL HELP

Some repairs aren't for the faint of heart or clumsy of hand. Say your idea of sewing on a button is taking the button and shirt to the seamstress at the dry-cleaners. You may not feel up to repairing the blown-out zipper on your $400 Gore-Tex jacket or the hole the cactus made in your tent floor. Fortunately, expert help is available—and it's not expensive.

Call first. Some manufacturers have procedures for returning and repairing damaged equipment, and if you don't follow their rules, they'll simply send your parcel back. Less frequently, manufacturers change addresses or merge with other companies. All major gear manufacturers are listed in *BACKPACKER* magazine's annual gear and apparel issues.

Warranties. Most major gear manufacturers, particularly those dealing in high-end gear, have excellent return policies for faulty equipment. The typical disclaimer is that gear is guaranteed against defects in workmanship and materials, not wear and tear; however, it's also true that in backpacking, wear and tear is the name of the game.

After all, the gear is supposedly designed (and definitely advertised) to withstand mega-abuse. Fortunately, most manufacturers do live up to their advertising: If the jacket you saw in an ad featuring a Himalayan expedition falls apart after a few trips, you can most likely have it repaired or replaced for free.

Repair specialists. You may have favorite old gear whose manufacturers have long since gone out of business. Or—as in the case of the boots I used to use—you may not trust the manufacturer to repair the equipment because you've had bad experiences in the past. Repair experts are listed in *BACKPACKER* magazine's annual gear issue. Call them first: Some have long waiting lists; others may not handle the specific repair you require. If you care about what the repair is going to cost, ask; it's not fair to start arguing about the price after the work has been done.

Clean gear first. It's actually a law in some states. If you don't clean your gear before putting it in a box and shipping it off, the repair facility may clean it for you—and charge for it.

Contact information. Write your name, address, and daytime phone number on a luggage tag and affix it to the gear. Even if you've previously described the problem on the phone, include in your package a note that describes as specifically as possible what you want done.

What to send. Send back only the part you need repaired. If your backpack's detachable waist belt has a split seam, there's no reason to ship off the whole pack.

Communicate your needs. Tell the manufacturer how you're using the gear—especially if you're doing something unusual. When they repair the gear, they may make an adaptation to suit you better, or they may recommend you buy something different next time.

SAVING LAND AND TRAIL

Record and report. Write to the local land management agency, the chamber of commerce, and the local hiking club and describe your trip. Mention observations both good and bad. With limited field staffs, land management agencies just might not know that that spring is dry or the trail overgrown. Tell the chamber of commerce why you came to the area (to visit its spectacular natural areas) and that you spent money at local businesses.

▲ ▲ ▲

Ten Ways to Keep in Touch with Nature

Much as we might like to, most of us can't live outdoors, or spend as much time in the backcountry as we would like. Here are ten ways to keep in touch with nature, even when the only tree in sight is the ficus in the corner of your office.

- Go out for a short overnight or a day hike. Not every trip has to be a major expedition. Even a few hours in the woods can be rejuvenating.
- Explore or volunteer to maintain a trail close to home. Lots of urban parks have hiking trails, which you can incorporate into your exercise routine.
- Attend a slide show about someone else's trip. (Places to find one include your local outfitters, an environmental organization, or a hiking club.)
- Give a talk at a local school. Bring in your tent, your stove, your backpacking food, and your water filter and share your expertise with the kids.
- Subscribe to an outdoors magazine to learn about new techniques, gear, and destinations.
- Plan your next trip. Get the maps, read the guidebooks, and learn about the area. When you get there, you'll feel like you've come home.
- Sign up for a class at a local nature center or park to learn more about the ecology close to home. You'll often find classes on everything from stargazing to mushroom hunting.
- Join an outings club and show up for a volunteer weekend.
- Hang out at your local outfitters. Check out the new gear, peruse the publications, and attend the slide shows.
- Hike in cyberspace. The Internet has tons of resources, including home pages, chat rooms, bulletin boards, and newsgroups for backpackers. Starting with *BACKPACKER* magazine's home page, you can cyber-hike all over the world!

Talk to locals. In some rural areas, local people are deeply suspicious of government programs, and trails get lumped into that category. In addition, locals often have the opinion that backpackers want to take land out of local use and production (timber and grazing operations), but that backpacking doesn't bring revenue into local communities. Patronize local businesses. If you stay at a hotel or eat in a restaurant, chat with the proprietors and let them know that you came to the area specifically to hike.

Take pictures. Share them with others. A good slide show can inspire others to hike in the area or just want to see it preserved.

Shots taken from far away or from an unusual perspective set hikers in the overall context (Photo: Jeff Scher © ERG)

Backlighting gives you the opportunity to present dramatic silhouettes. (Photo: ©Karen Berger/Daniel R. Smith)

Designation signs will remind you of the names of trails and help set the scene for viewers (Photo: ©Karen Berger/Daniel R. Smith)

Close-ups present an intimate view of nature and help bring home details of your trip. (Photo: ©Karen Berger/Daniel R. Smith)

Stop in at land management agencies. Land management agencies need to know who's using the trails. Plus, you'll pick up the most current information.

Get on a mailing list. Ask if there's an organization working to protect the area (a hiking club, an environmental group, or a natural history association). Join these organizations: It's an effective, low-cost way to give back to the trail and keep informed with issues that pertain to it.

Write letters to the editor. Let local people know about the trail you hiked, what was special about it, and that it's the reason you'll be returning to their communities to spend tourist dollars.

Participate. The public comment period for government planning for such projects as new roads, timber sales, and wilderness designation is your chance to be heard on the subject of how your public lands are managed. These letters and comments make a very real difference, particularly on federal lands, where recreation is usually written into the management plan of an area.

Volunteer. Trail clubs are volunteer-staffed operations, and they need help in everything from writing an article for the newsletter to

Volunteering is a great way to keep in touch with and help out your fellow backpackers. Here, the author helps install a latrine on the Appalachian Trail. (Photo: ©Karen Berger/Daniel R. Smith)

swinging a Pulaski on the trail. Sign up. If you don't, you have no room to complain the next time you find yourself crawling over deadfall because the maintaining group hasn't yet finished clearing the debris from a recent storm.

Show up. Attending organized events like National Trails Day and local activities like a ribbon-cutting ceremony to designate a new trail shows public officials that people care about hiking trails. And it rewards the volunteers who keep the trails open for all of us.

Experienced hikers know their most important piece of gear isn't some nifty doodad—it's the gray matter they carry in their heads. (Photo: ©Jeff Scher)

Index

altitude sickness, 157-58
animals
    food precautions, 75, 85-90
    gear storage/damage control, 86
    mice, in shelters, 85-87
    porcupines, 86
    See also bear country
Appalachian Trail, 15, 27, 57, 68
    shelters, 84-85
    through-hikers, 37, 57

backpacks
    balancing load, 20
    care and storage, 25-27, 190
    compression sacks, 120
    external-frame, 116, 178
    fit/trial run, 16
    internal-frame, 16, 140
    keeping lightweight, 8, 10, 14-17, 21-22, 32
    overnight/animal intruders, 86
    pack covers, 24, 30, 112, 115, 116
    repairs, 175, 178, 180-81, 190
    security/locks, 28
    sharing gear, 15-16, 21-22, 93-94
    small containers, 21
    spill prevention, 27, 51
    stuff sacks, 17, 19-20, 24, 64, 110-11, 116
    unnecessary features, 16
    waist belt/buckles, 23, 64, 86, 175, 180-81
    waterproofing/buoyancy, 64
    wearing when lost, 69-70
backpacks, air travel with
    checking as luggage, 26-28
    stove/fuel/weight restrictions, 27-28
    travel-proofing, 25-28
backpacks, packing and organizing, 17, 19-21, 91-92, 102
    packing out garbage, 97-98
    rainy weather, 110-11, 115-16
    in shelters, 85
    stoves/fuel, 26, 105
bandannas, 23, 98, 123, 143, 144-45, 164
bathing/personal hygiene, 21, 95-97, 148, 154
bear country
    black bears, 87, 89
    food precautions/bear-bagging, 24, 53, 54, 75, 88-90, 91
    grizzlies, 32, 87, 89-90, 97
    menstruation in, 97
birdwatching, 94
books, 93-94

boots
    blisters/prevention, 126, 131-34
    care and storage, 182, 188-89
    cold/winter weather, 117-18
    drying, 182
    fit/breaking in, 16, 131-33, 134, 179
    laces/innersoles, 23, 131-32
    overnight/animal intruders, 86
    repairs, 177, 181-82, 188
    wet/muddy conditions, 66, 71, 112-13

campfires, 72-73, 143, 145
    burning garbage, 98
    for cooking, 7-8, 100-03, 143
    dung fire, 7-8
    environmental impact, 72, 73, 100-01
    matches/fuel, 102-03
    safety, 143
    for signaling, 102, 159
camp kitchen
    animal-proofing/bear-bagging, 24, 85-86, 87-91
    cookfires, 7-8, 101-03, 143
    cooking gear, 19, 22, 35, 85, 99-100, 103-07, 108
    cleanup/sanitation, 47, 53, 85, 99, 108, 154
    low-impact tips, 95, 101, 108
    rainy-day cooking, 35, 38, 106-07
    siting, 90-91, 104
    See also garbage; stoves
campsite, 74
    activities, 93-95
    animal-proofing, 85-91
    choosing, 74-79, 90-91, 97
    designated/established, 75, 76-77
    hazards, 77
    low-impact tips, 75-77, 78, 91, 95, 96-97
    soils/sleeping surface, 75-77, 81
    See also camp kitchen; garbage; tents; waste, human
candles, 92, 103
car
    packing keys, 20-21, 25
    security/trailhead parking, 25
chair. *See* seats
cheesecloth, 24, 145, 164
clothing, 22
    care and storage, 186-87, 191-93
    cold/winter weather, 17, 119-23
    fabrics, 122, 133, 186-87
    fit/trial run, 16
    gaiters, 60, 113, 136, 149, 151, 188
    gloves, 114, 121

hats, 112, 121-23
hot weather, 123, 142
mouse damage, 86
outerwear, 119-20
packing and organizing, 110-11
rain gear, 22, 24, 111, 112-13, 114-16, 122, 151, 177, 186-87, 192, 194
repairs, 177, 193, 194
socks, 114, 120, 121, 122, 131, 133, 135, 146, 149
vapor-barrier liners, 121, 122
washing/drying, 24, 96-97, 113, 114, 115, 133, 146, 155, 186-87
cold-weather/winter camping, 117-23
gear for, 63, 82, 116, 118-19, 173, 188
hiking tips, 62-64
hypothermia, 128-29, 136, 144, 155-56
pitching/staking tent, 82
poisonous plants, 150
pull cords/locks, for cold fingers, 193
staying warm, 107, 117-23
water supply, 166, 172-74
compass, 68-69
cooking gear. *See* camp kitchen
cord, uses, 24, 88, 90, 171, 177, 193
pulls and locks, 193

dehydration, 156-57, 161, 166-67
drinks, 47-49
alcoholic, 45, 47, 128
bouillon, 45
coffee/tea, 47-49
cold, 123
cups/mugs for, 100, 102
hot, 45, 47-49, 100, 102, 120, 122, 156
hydration, 47, 59, 125, 155, 156, 158, 161-62, 164, 166
powdered, 49
wine, 47, 49
See also water supply
duct tape, 177, 179, 181-82
See also repair kit

environmental impact. *See* low-impact camping, tips for

fanny pack
necessities pouch, 21, 114
fires. *See* campfires
first aid, 127-28
altitude sickness, 158
ankle problems, 141
blisters, 23, 134-37
bug bites and stings, 147-48
burns, 128, 130, 143-44
course, 128, 130-31
cuts and wounds, 128, 141-42
dislocated shoulder, 141

evacuation and rescue, 144, 153, 159
falls, sprains, and strains, 140-41
fractures/splints, 140
friction rashes, 142
gastrointestinal illness, 154-55, 167
hyperthermia/dehydration, 156-57, 167
hypothermia, 129, 156
knee problems, 141
musculoskeletal problems, 137-38
poisonous plant rashes, 151-52
shock, 153
snakebite, 129, 153
tick bites, 149
tourniquets, 128
See also injuries/illnesses, prevention
first-aid kit, 22, 129-31, 133, 136, 137, 140-41, 148, 151, 152, 178
fishing, 53
flashlight, 92-93
batteries, 17, 92-93, 191
food
animal-proofing/bear-bagging, 24, 85-86, 87-91
breads, 40, 41
butter/spreads, 42, 51
canned, 40, 44
cheese, 41
condiments, 46
containers, 45-46, 51
convenience vs. creativity, 34-36
dehydrating, 42-45
eggs, 42
estimating quantities, 35-36, 45, 51-52
fish, 42, 43-44, 53
freeze-dried, 7, 34-35, 38, 40
fresh foods, 34, 35, 41-42
fruit, 41, 43-44, 53-55
for gastrointestinal illness recovery, 154
meats, 41, 42, 43-44
menu planning, 35-36
noodles/pasta, 38-39, 40, 105
nutrition/calories, 36-38, 59, 111
packing and packaging, 45-46, 49-51
prepackaged dinners, 39-41, 50
resupplying/food drops, 30-32, 52
rice/grains, 39
sauces, 38-39, 43-44, 45-47
seasonings/spices, 34, 45-47
snacks, 37, 40, 53-54, 59, 111, 114
soups/stews, 38, 44, 46, 55
sprouts, 34, 42
staples, 38-41
weight, 22, 35
wild/foraging, 51-55, 194
See also camp kitchen
footwear
boots, 67, 71, 112-13, 117-18, 126, 131-34, 147
camp shoes, 66-67, 78-79, 134, 147

cold/winter weather, 117-18, 120, 121, 188
  gaiters, 60, 113, 136, 149, 151, 188
  river crossings, 66, 79
  socks, 114, 120, 121, 122, 131, 133, 135, 149
  vapor barrier liners, 121, 122
  wet/muddy conditions, 66, 71, 112-14

gaiters, 60, 113, 136, 149, 151, 188
games, 94-95
garbage
  burning, 98
  disposal, 47, 53, 97-98
  from menstruation, 97-98
  minimizing, 50
  packing out, 97-98
garbage bags, uses, 24, 64, 112, 115-16, 117, 172
gear and equipment
  battery-powered, 17, 92-93, 117, 191
  care/storage, 186-95
  checklist, 191
  for cold-weather/winter camping, 60, 63, 82,
    116, 118-19, 173
  comforts and amenities, 91-95
  cooking gear, 21-22, 35, 85, 99-100, 103-07, 108
  DEET cautions, 144
  essential, 7-8, 18, 93, 100, 102-03, 114-15, 119,
    121-22, 130-31, 177
  carrying capacity/pack weight, 15, 22
  keeping lightweight, 8, 10, 13, 15-17, 22, 32, 130
  multi-use items, 16-17, 23-24
  packing and organizing, 19-22, 85, 91-92, 110-
    11, 115
  repairs, 23, 175-76, 179-85, 187-88, 190, 194-95
  resupplying, 30-32
  sharing, 15-16, 21-22, 93-94
  used, 178-79
  warranties/returns, 194-95
  waterproofing/rain protection, 110-11, 115
  zippers, 177-78, 180, 194
ground cloth, 24, 82-83, 84, 115, 125, 172
group trips
  environmental impact, 70-71

hammock, 83-84, 189
headlamp, 92
hiking
  balance/controlling a fall, 139-40
  direction, 125
  fitness/training, 137-38
  navigation, 67-70
  losing/finding trail, 67-68, 69-70, 102
  low-impact tips, 70-73
  pace/mileage limits, 58-59, 137-38
  rests, 59, 138, 157
  in rain, 66, 110-15
  river crossings, 64-67, 79
  scree, 60-61, 138

snow and ice, 62-64, 69
  talus, 60-62
  See also trails; weather
hiking sticks/trekking poles, 24, 56, 62, 65-66, 83,
  116, 125, 138-41, 152
hot weather/climates, 123-25, 142
  heat exhaustion, 156-57
  heat stroke, 157
hunting season, precautions, 28-30

ice
  crampons, 60, 63
  hiking techniques, 62-63
  ice ax, 63, 82, 116
  staking tent, 82
illnesses. *See* injuries/illnesses, prevention
information, sources of, 12-14
  guidebooks, 12-14, 17, 94
  hiking clubs, 12, 25, 179
  Internet, 13, 194
  land management agencies, 13-14, 25, 58, 198
  maps, 12-14, 25, 74
  outfitters, 12, 179
injuries/illnesses, prevention, 127-28
  altitude sickness, 157-57
  ankle problems, 138-40
  blisters, 60, 126, 127, 131-34
  bug bites and stings, 144-47
  burns, 143
  cuts and wounds, 141
  falls, sprains, and strains, 138-40
  friction rashes, 142
  frostbite, 121, 177
  gastrointestinal illnesses, 161-66
  hyperthermia/dehydration, 47, 59, 125, 144,
    155, 156-57, 158, 161, 166-67
  hypothermia, 128, 144, 155
  knee problems, 24, 56, 137, 138-40
  musculoskeletal problems, 137-38, 140
  mushroom poisoning, 54-55
  poisonous plant rashes, 150-51
  snakebite, 152-53
  tendinitis, 138
  tick bites, 148-49
  See also first aid
insects, 80
  bite treatments, 147-48
  protection against, 145-47
  repellents/DEET, 144-45, 149
  stings, 147-48
  ticks, 148-49
itinerary, 28-29, 33

knife, pocket, 100, 141, 177

light. *See* candles; flashlight; headlamp
lost hiker, 67-68, 69-70, 102

See also signaling
low-impact camping, tips for
 campfires, 101
 campsite selection, 75-77
 erosion/trails, 70-73
 sanitation/waste disposal, 95, 101, 108
 wild-food foraging, 52-53

maps
 creating your own trail from, 13-14, 25
 finding campsites, 74-75
 folding, 20
 other uses, 68
 trimming, 17   •
 types/sources, 12-14, 25
money/credit cards, packing, 20-21
mushrooms, wild, 54-55, 194
music, 94

national parks
 bear problems, 87, 88
 search and rescue, 127
National Park Service
 trail information/maps, 13-14, 25, 58
nature, experiencing
 between trips, 193-94
 group size and, 70-71
navigating
 by GPS, 69
 by map and compass, 68-69
 natural direction signs, 68, 70

packs. *See* backpacks; fanny pack
partner, hiking with, 15-16, 21-22
 first aid, 156, 158
 losing/finding trail, 69-70, 72
 massage, 134, 138
 pace, 58
 reading aloud, 93-94
 sharing gear, 15-16, 21-22, 93-94, 141
personal hygiene, 95-98
photography/slides, 194, 196-97
pillows, 17, 92
plants
 identification, 94
 poisonous, 150-51
 wild edible, 52-55, 194

rain
 cooking in, 35, 38, 106-07
 hiking in, 66, 110-15
 protection from, 77-78, 80-81, 84-85, 115-16
 wet/dry clothing, 10-11, 113, 114, 115, 116,
   133, 155
rain gear, 22, 24, 111, 112-13, 114-16, 122, 151
 care and storage, 186-87, 192
 repairs, 177, 194

repair kit, 23-24, 176-78, 182
 spares, 178
repairs
 boots, 177, 181-82
 field, 175-76, 179-85
 gluing, 177, 181-82
 mattress, 177, 179-80, 183
 packs, 175, 178, 180-81, 190
 patching and taping, 23, 176-78, 179-80, 183
 tent/poles, 177-78, 179-80, 183-85
 zippers, 177-78, 180, 194
rescue. *See* search and rescue
rivers, crossing, 64-67, 79
 current, 64-66
 snow bridges, 66
rocks
 balance/controlling falls, 139-40
 dislodged/falling, 61, 77
 hiking over scree, 60-61
 hiking over talus, 60-62
 snake cautions, 152
 storm cautions, 116

safety, 127
 hunting season, 28-30
 planning for, 28-30, 32-33
 strangers, 28
 winter camping, 119
scorpions, 147
search and rescue, 127
 cost/insurance, 28-29
 evacuation, 144, 153, 159
 See also signaling
seat
 foam pad, 18, 90, 122
 folding portable chair, 90
shelters (lean-tos)
 etiquette, 85
 packing and organizing gear, 85
 rodents/animal pests, 85-87
 weatherproofing, 84-85
showers, 95-96
signaling
 with fires, 102, 159
 with mirror, 68-69
 with whistle, 24, 32
sleeping bag, 22, 129
 cleaning and storage, 95, 189
 cold weather, 117-18, 120
 hot weather, 147
 keeping dry, 111, 115
 liners, 95, 120
 packing, 111
 repairs/zippers, 177-78, 180, 194
sleeping pad, 22, 122, 123
 closed-cell foam, recycling, 19, 24, 123, 174
 inflatable foam mattress, 64, 91, 101, 177, 190

repairs, 177, 179-80, 183, 190
snakes, 152-53
   snakebite treatment, 153
snow
   hiking tips, 62-64
   staking tent, 82
soap, 96-97
   containers for, 21
solo trips
   vs. hiking with partner, 15-16, 21-22
   precautions, 28-30, 32-33, 69-71
   tent site, 79
stargazing, 94, 194
storms. *See* weather
stoves, 19, 21, 27, 103-06
   cleaning and storage, 190-91
   cold/winter weather, 117
   cooking/operating tips, 99, 103-07
   efficiency/fuel consumption, 103, 105-06, 163
   fuels/bottles, 7-8, 21, 23, 27, 103-07, 117, 143,
      163, 177, 190
   packing, 21, 23
   priming, 23, 104, 107, 143
   repairs and maintenance, 177, 191
   safety, 143
stuff sacks, 17, 19-20, 117, 192
   garbage bags as, 24, 64
   waterproof, 19-20, 64, 110-11, 116
sun protection, 119, 123-25, 143

tarps, 24, 82-83, 125, 171
tents, 22
   alternative, 81, 83, 84-85
   care and storage, 144, 187, 192
   cold/winter camping, 117-19, 123
   cooking caveats, 106-07, 143
   guying/staking, 24, 81-82, 115, 183, 193
   packing, 23, 111
   pitching, 79-80, 115
   rain precautions, 79-80, 81
   repairs, 177-78, 179-80, 183-85, 194
   seam-sealing/waterproofing, 187-88
   in shelters, 85
   siting/orienting, 75-77, 79-81, 98-91, 117
   ventilation/condensation, 79-80, 117, 184
   See also ground cloth
time of day, telling, 68
trails
   blazes/cairns, 67, 70-72
   blowdowns, 71-72
   choosing, 58
   creating your own, 14-15, 25
   elevation gain, 58, 137-38, 157
   information, 58
   loop hikes, 25
   losing/finding, 67-68, 69, 71, 102
   maintaining, 71-73, 194-96

   mileage, 14, 58-59
   mud, 69, 71
   registers/signing in, 28-29
   respect for property rights, 73
   shortcuts, 71-72
   switchbacks, 71
   water bars, 71
   See also hiking

U.S. Forest Service
   trail information/maps, 13-14, 25, 58

warm, staying, 117-23
   clothing, 119-23
   drinks/hot water, 120, 122, 163, 174
   footwear, 117-18, 120, 121
   sleeping bag/bedding, 117-18, 120
waste, human
   disposal, 95, 97-98
water filters, 22, 24, 164-66
   cleaning, 165-66, 191
water supply, 22, 47, 129, 154, 162, 168-73
   boiling, 163, 173
   cold-weather/winter camping, 172-73
   Cryptosporidium, 163
   filtering, 22, 24, 164-66
   Giardia, 129, 154, 162-64, 172
   hard-to-reach, 24, 171
   hot springs, 173
   hot water, 105, 143
   iodine, 163-64
   low-impact tips, 75-76, 96-97
   purification, 154, 162-66, 173
   solar still, 172
   washing/bathing, 75-76, 96-97
   water bottles/bags, 18-19, 24, 166, 167-68, 171,
      173, 174, 193
   See also dehydration; drinks
weather
   cold/freezing, 62-64, 82, 114, 117-23
   forecasting, 110-11
   hot, 123-25, 142, 156-57
   lightning, 116-17
   patterns, 80
   rain, 35, 38, 66, 77-78, 80-81, 84-85, 106-07,
      109-16
   snow and ice, 62-64, 82, 117-19
   storms and wind, 35, 77-78, 80-81, 84-85, 117, 172
   See also cold-weather/winter camping; hot
     weather/climates; rain; wind
wind, 110
   fire cautions, 101
   protection from, 77-78, 80-81, 84-85, 117
winter camping. *See* cold-weather/winter camping;
   ice; snow
women
   hygiene/menstruation, 97-98

About the Author

A contributing editor at *BACKPACKER* magazine, Karen Berger has hiked more than 10,000 miles on five continents, including the Appalachian Trail, the Continental Divide Trail, and the Pacific Coast Trail. With her husband and hiking partner, Daniel R. Smith, she coauthored *Where the Waters Divide: A Walk Along America's Continental Divide*. She has written widely about travel, fitness, outdoor adventure, and the environment.